DATE DUE			

3930012869

921
FULTON

Landau, Elaine.

Robert Fulton.

PRAIRIE VIEW JUNIOR HIGH
TINLEY PARK IL 60477

319477 01240   07395B   27

ROBERT FULTON

ROBERT FULTON

BY ELAINE LANDAU

A FIRST BOOK   FRANKLIN WATTS   NEW YORK/LONDON/TORONTO/SYDNEY/1991

Cover photographs courtesy of: New York Public Library, Picture Collection and Historical Pictures Service, Inc.

Photographs courtesy of: AP/Wide World Photos: p. 13; New York Public Library, Picture Collection: pp. 16, 17, 22, 23, 27, 29, 31, 36, 39, 44, 46, 47, 50, 52; The Bettmann Archive: pp. 20, 56; Historical Picture Service: pp. 2, 3, 28, 33, 34, 35, 40, 41, 49, 53, 55.

Library of Congress Cataloging-in-Publication Data

Landau, Elaine.
Robert Fulton / Elaine Landau.
p.   cm.—(A First book)
Includes bibliographical references and index.
Summary: Describes the life and work of the talented inventor and resourceful businessman, with special emphasis on his development of the steamboat.
ISBN 0-531-20016-7
1. Fulton, Robert, 1765–1815—Juvenile literature.   2. Marina
Engineers—United States—Biography—Juvenile literature.
3. Inventors—United States—Biography—Juvenile literature.
4. Steamboats—United States—History—19th century—Juvenile
literature.   5. Steamboats—History—19th century—Juvenile
literature.   [1. Fulton, Robert, 1765–1815.   2. Inventors.
3. Steamboats—History.]   I. Title.   II. Series.
VM140.F9L33   1991
623.8'24'092   B—dc20   90-47865
CIP
AC

CONTENTS

For May and Charles Brennan

THE EARLY YEARS

It all began on a golden autumn day on a large country farm in Little Britain Township, Pennsylvania. On November 14, 1765, a baby boy with dark, curly hair was born to Robert and Mary Smith Fulton. Although the couple already had three children, this was their first son. They named the boy Robert after his father.

Robert Fulton, Jr., had been born into an upstanding family. In addition to running the farm, Mr. Fulton was active in the First Presbyterian Church. He was also among the first members of the local Juliana Library—the third oldest library in America.

The baby's mother was a hardworking, thoughtful woman. Mary Smith Fulton ran the house, helped her husband, and cared for their three daughters and young son. Mrs. Fulton's favorite hobby was gardening. She spent much of her spare time tending the rows of colorful blossoms she had planted.

The Fultons' farm spanned 394 acres. The family lived in a two-story, solidly build house of gray stone. Young Robert enjoyed growing up in the lush green countryside. He and his sisters especially liked playing outdoors. The young boy loved wildflowers, farm animals, and wading in the creek that ran past their property.

Yet before long, things began to go badly for the Fulton family. Young Robert's parents had bought the farm just a year before his birth. Its purchase left them heavily in debt.

In addition, Mr. Fulton wasn't an experienced farmer. A combination of poor soil and bad weather

Robert Fulton was born in this house. Today his family's home is open to the public as a museum.

resulted in a string of unprofitable farm years. Numerous hailstorms had destroyed crops and killed much of the farm's poultry. And nearly all the animal pens were destroyed.

By the time Robert turned six, his family was forced to sell the farm. Since they'd borrowed so much money, nearly everything the Fultons owned had to be sold at a sheriff's sale. Their various possessions were publicly auctioned off for whatever price they would bring. Robert Jr. tearfully watched as even the family's cooking pots and his own bed were sold to strangers. The family members had been permitted to keep only their clothing.

At that point, Robert Jr.'s life changed greatly. The Fultons moved back to Lancaster, Pennsylvania, where they had lived before buying the farm. The growing and bustling town of Lancaster was nothing like the quiet farm where Robert Jr. had been born. Lancaster had over four thousand residents and five hundred houses. There were numerous taverns and all sorts of shops and businesses.

Robert Sr. ran a tailoring shop. He had been known as a good tailor before he had tried his hand at farming. Now Mr. Fulton did well once again. Soon he took on an apprentice, a young helper who learned the tailoring trade as he worked at Fulton's side.

But before long, misfortune again struck the family. Only two years after they had returned to Lancaster, Robert Sr. suddenly became ill and died. Despite his success in business, he hadn't put aside very much money. Once again, the Fultons found themselves nearly penniless.

Now it was up to Robert Jr.'s mother to do what she could to provide for the family and educate her children. A few relatives tried to help by offering small amounts of money. Things would be difficult. Before her husband's death, Mrs. Fulton had given birth to a second son. This meant there were five children to care for.

In spite of the financial hardships, Robert's childhood was still filled with many happy moments. All the children looked forward to delicious holiday dinners at their relatives' homes. As a young boy, Robert especially enjoyed reading. In fact, his room was usually filled with a wide assortment of books and magazines.

When Robert turned eight, Mrs. Fulton managed to send him to a private school. He was not an outstanding student but showed promise in some areas. Robert proved to be a quick-thinking boy. Often he would point out new and interesting ways to complete everyday tasks.

When Robert was only ten, he began collecting

Robert Fulton's birthplace, shown here, is located about 22 miles south of Lancaster, Pennsylvania. Today Lancaster is one of the richest farming areas in the nation as well as an important manufacturing center.

whatever scraps of sheet metal he was able to find. Then he hammered out the lead contained in the sheets and used it to fashion his own pencils for writing and drawing.

At thirteen, young Fulton saved Lancaster's Independence Day celebration. Candles had been in short supply at the time of the event. As a result, the town council had forbidden their use in the July Fourth festivities. To make up for the lack of brightness, Robert invented a blazing sky rocket. The glowing cone-shaped missile soared upward as the crowds cheered.

Robert created other devices as well. Although he enjoyed fishing with his friends in nearby lakes and streams, he disliked having to row the boat. To improve these outings, Fulton fashioned mechanical rowing paddles to help propel the boat through the water.

Young Fulton conducted all sorts of experiments in his spare time. He enjoyed trying out new methods and spent months experimenting with mercury. He became so involved in these trials that his young friends teased him and nicknamed him "Quicksilver Bob." All this took place years before schools ever held science fairs!

Robert also liked to draw and paint. By the time he had turned thirteen, he had done both landscapes and portraits. The young boy's work showed remarkable skill and clarity.

However, as the years passed, Robert had less time for boyhood hobbies. When he was fifteen, his family felt that he should learn a trade. They tried to think of the best way for him to earn a living. Silversmiths were highly regarded at the time, and Robert's relatives thought the boy's artistic ability might be helpful in metalwork. So Robert was apprenticed to a silversmith.

But young Fulton soon found he didn't enjoy the work. He later told a friend that he disliked nearly everything about being an apprentice. The talented boy not only resented his low position, he also hated having to copy other people's work.

Nevertheless, Robert acquired some valuable skills as an apprenticed silversmith. He had an opportunity to study design and metalwork and also learned how a successful business is run.

Though busy as an apprenticed silversmith, Robert still found some hours in which to continue his painting. He sold several portraits and saved whatever little money came his way. After two years, Fulton was finally able to buy his way out of his apprenticeship.

Now, at seventeen, Robert decided to devote himself to his art. He moved to Philadelphia,

*Here a silversmith designs jewelry
and other items. Fulton learned
these skills as an apprentice.*

where, as a young artist, he did very well. He sold oil portraits and watercolor landscapes as well as very small paintings called miniatures. At times, he even did some silversmithing to increase his income.

Before long, he had saved up a small sum of money and was at last able to help his mother and family. While growing up, Robert Fulton, Jr., had remained a devoted son. He knew that his mother had often gone without things so that he could attend school, have books, and enjoy his boyhood.

He wanted to be sure she would be comfortable in her old age. Robert knew how badly his mother had felt when they lost their farm and the lovely garden she had so enjoyed. In fact, it was Mary Smith Fulton who had urged her husband to leave the city. She believed the countryside was a better place to raise a family.

Robert Jr. wanted to make his mother's dream come true again, so he purchased a small but beautiful farm in a quiet part of Pennsylvania. He made certain that there was a spot for a garden behind the house. Years later, he would tell a friend about the tears of joy in his mother's eyes when he handed her the property deed.

Fulton often worked long hours to achieve his goals. But after a while, the hard work took a toll on

As a young artist Fulton lived in the lively
city of Philadelphia, shown here. Philadelphia
is especially important historically, as both
the Declaration of Independence and the
U.S. Constitution were adopted there.

*This color portrait of Robert Fulton
as a young man was painted
by Rembrandt Peale, one of
young Fulton's good friends.*

his health. By the time he turned twenty-one, he had become seriously ill. His lungs were inflamed and he had begun to spit up blood. He might have actually been suffering from tuberculosis, which was then quite common in Philadelphia.

At the time, Fulton tried a number of the most commonly used cures. These included adding large amounts of prunes and large doses of salt to his diet. He also exercised more and visited a resort known for its fresh mountain air.

Finally, Fulton was advised to go abroad. He hoped to improve both his health and his skill as a painter in Europe. Fulton knew that Europe was a center for the arts, and that many young artists had become famous there. In 1786, young Robert Fulton set sail for London, England. At the time, he never imagined that this new adventure would separate him from his home and family in Pennsylvania for nearly twenty years.

THE YEARS ABROAD

Robert Fulton found that being an unknown artist in London could be difficult. Europe was filled with struggling artists like himself. For his first year abroad, Fulton had hoped to live off his savings. However, it was often hard to make ends meet.

Robert Fulton searched for inexpensive rooms to live in. He also gratefully accepted dinner invitations extended to him by more successful artists. Fulton was especially fortunate to be befriended by Benjamin West, an American painter who had become famous in Europe. At times, Fulton felt tired and discouraged. He also missed his family in

America, even more so because in those days it took many months to receive an overseas letter.

While in London, Fulton experimented with different painting methods and tried working on larger canvases. He also completed a self-portrait that he sent to his mother.

Although Fulton actually achieved some small success as an artist, he never lost his interest in inventing things. He had arrived in England during the Industrial Revolution. Nearly everywhere he looked, Fulton saw new inventions and machines. Factories were springing up throughout London as well as in other areas. Roadways, canals, and bridges were being designed to connect manufacturers, warehouses, and merchants. It was an exciting time for a young man who had always been fascinated by machines and new ways to do things.

Even as Fulton supported himself as an artist, he closely followed various engineering projects with keen interest. He traveled throughout Europe, meeting with inventors as well as investors interested in supporting new projects. He was anxious to learn all he could. He spent many hours studying math and science. As he traveled, he also became fluent in German, Italian, and French.

After a time, Robert Fulton put some of his ideas down on paper. He designed a system of small ca-

*Fulton painted this oil portrait of himself.
Painted on a canvas that measured 30
inches by 25 inches, the painting was shipped
from Europe to America as a gift to Fulton's mother.*

*Left: In Europe, Fulton showed others his designs
for new projects. Before long, Fulton's intense
interest in science and industry outweighed
his love for the art world.*

*Above: Canals such as this one in England greatly
interested Fulton. He wanted to begin similar
projects in America, and while in Europe he had
written to both General George Washington
and the governor of Pennsylvania about his ideas.*

nals that he believed could improve commerce. Fulton felt that businesses using his system might transport their goods more easily. He insisted that his canal system could accomplish more work with fewer people.

There were other inventions as well. Three of Fulton's machines received a great deal of acclaim. One device was especially useful in the textile industry. This machine speedily spun flax into linen. Fulton also invented a device to twist hemp into rope. Among his better-known inventions was a machine that sawed large slabs of marble into manageable pieces. Fulton was later awarded a silver medal from Europe's Society for the Encouragement of Arts, Commerce, and Manufactures for his design.

Robert Fulton's inventions mirrored his broad range of interests. However, one binding thread connected much of his work. Robert Fulton had long been concerned with water and sea vessels. While still a young man in America, Fulton had designed a mechanical paddle for a rowboat. Now years later, in 1797, he perfected a design for a submarine. Fulton had realized early on that submarines could be useful in naval warfare. Even his early experimental models dived beneath the water and quickly resurfaced.

*Oxen draw marble into a shop for carving.
Years before, while in Europe, Fulton had invented
an award-winning marble-cutting device.*

Fulton never achieved true success with his submarine, *Nautilus*, possibly because he lacked the funds to do his best work. Money was difficult to come by. Fulton tried approaching France with his submarine project during an extended visit there. Since France was at war with England, he thought the French might be interested.

The young inventor succeeded in attracting the attention of the French emperor, Napoleon. The emperor appointed a committee of experts to study Fulton's work. They asked Fulton to prove the *Nautilus*'s merit by having it destroy an enemy British ship. If Fulton succeeded, Napoleon agreed to pay him handsomely. Not only would Fulton's expenses in designing and building the submarine be covered but there would also be a fair sum of money left over.

Although Fulton spent an entire summer trying, he wasn't able to accomplish the feat Napoleon proposed. As a result, he didn't receive a penny for all his work. Napoleon's committee also made it clear that they were no longer interested in Fulton's ideas.

Robert Fulton's hopes collapsed. Yet before long, things began to improve. England had heard about Fulton's submarine and its attempts to overtake their vessel. When they learned that he was no

A drawing of Fulton's first submarine, the Nautilus. *This vessel could carry five passengers and remain underwater for eight hours.*

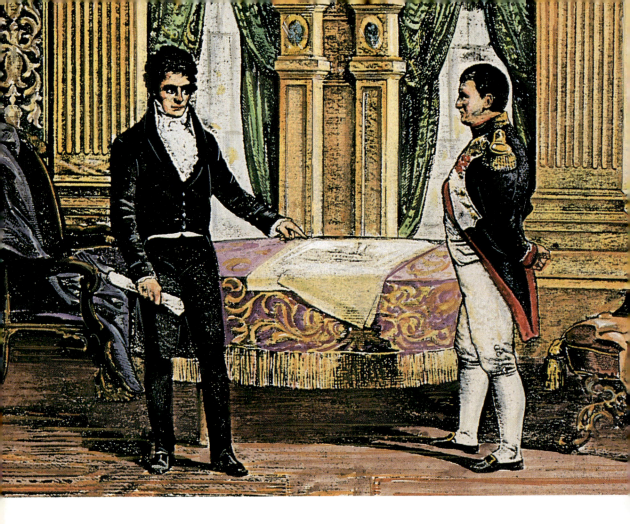

*Above: Fulton and Napoleon discuss working as a team.
Napoleon, who had crowned himself emperor of France,
had created a vast empire. As Napoleon was of below-
average height, early on he had been nicknamed
"the little corporal." Right: Fulton tries out an
early steamboat in Paris on the Seine River. After
it sank, Fulton went on to build an
improved, successful model.*

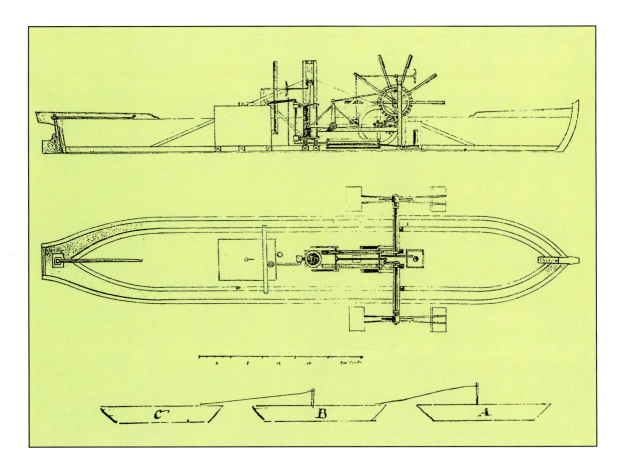

*Fulton's drawings of the steamboat
he hoped to build show his attention
to detail, form, and design.*

longer working with France, British representatives approached him.

They encouraged Fulton to side with them against France. The British agreed to experiments with self-propelled underwater missiles, known as torpedoes. But, although Fulton launched several torpedo attacks against French vessels, no ships were sunk.

The following year Fulton finally proved that the torpedo could be a useful wartime weapon when a test site target was successfully blown up. But by then the British had lost interest. So, at that point, Fulton's success actually mattered little. While he had dealt with these European nations, Robert Fulton had kept American officials aware of his work and progress. But the United States could not find a use for the *Nautilus* either.

However, soon Fulton's exceptional talent would enrich his own country. The opportunity arose when he met an American in Europe named Robert R. Livingston. Mr. Livingston had long dreamed of having steamboats navigate America's waterways. In fact, by the time Livingston met Fulton, he had already obtained a New York state monopoly for steamboating. This meant that Livingston had the sole right to operate steamboats on New York's waterways.

Livingston had the opportunity and the financial resources to bring steamboating to New York. All he needed was a bright creative engineer to design and oversee the construction of a workable vessel. Livingston found exactly what he had been looking for in Robert Fulton.

Fulton's longtime interest in water travel made him an excellent choice for the task. Fulton was filled with enthusiasm in the fall of 1802 as he set to work on the project. By spring of the following year, Fulton had finished the vessel's construction. As he was still in Europe at the time, he tried the steamboat out on a river there.

But Fulton's hopes and expectations sank along with the boat as he watched it splinter into pieces on the water and go down to the river's bottom. As Fulton now realized, the vessel's working parts had been too heavy for its frame.

Yet he refused to give up. Fulton went to work improving his steamboat's design. By the summer of 1803, he had produced a superior vessel. This time the trial run was a success. Propelled by the force of steam, the boat moved smoothly through the water.

Fulton was thrilled with the results. Now more than ever, he longed to return to America. He was filled with all sorts of ideas about how steamboats

*In this oil painting, Robert Fulton (right)
explains plans for his first steamboat to
backer Robert R. Livingston. The two later
achieved financial success as well as
a useful service for travelers.*

could improve travel in the United States. He also hoped that his plans for inland canals might be used in America.

As it turned out, Fulton had to wait nearly two years before he returned to his homeland. This was partly due to the difficulties he experienced in trying to export a steam engine. The British government had placed a ban on taking steam engines out of the country. The British had enjoyed a boom in commerce as a result of the Industrial Revolution.

Now they didn't want to export British machinery, fearing that other nations might copy their designs and create trade competition.

It took Fulton nearly two years to persuade the British government to allow him to bring a single steam engine to the United States. He also spent a good deal of time urging the British manufacturer to complete the engine's construction. Finally in the fall of 1806, everything was ready. Robert Fulton boarded a ship for America.

This canal in Oswego, New York, built after Fulton's death, represents the type of advanced canal work Fulton longed to do while he lived. He had even written a book filled with detailed illustrations of how small canals could improve water transportation.

41

RETURNING HOME

Fulton's voyage home took about two months. Upon arriving, he was glad to plant his feet on American soil. Almost immediately, Fulton began working on a new steamboat. He hired a famous New York shipbuilder to help construct the vessel.

As Fulton had hoped, it proved to be an impressive vessel. The steamboat was 133 feet (40.5 m) long and 18 feet (5.5 m) wide. The steam engine rested uncovered in the front portion of the vessel. The engine's working parts could be plainly seen and admired by observers. There were also two large paddle wheels on the boat's sides. Contrary to popular belief, there is no evidence that Fulton named his vessel the *Clermont*.

The steamboat's launch date was set for August 17, 1807. It was an exciting time for everyone connected with the project but especially for Robert Fulton, who, for so long, had dreamed of that day. Fulton, along with a crowd of others, anxiously watched as the steamboat began its 150-mile (240-km) run. Fortunately, everything went as planned. The boat regally sailed up the Hudson River from New York City to the capital of New York State at Albany.

With black puffs of smoke rising from its stacks, the boat reached its destination in twenty-four hours. Then it turned around to return home. Fulton's steamboat traveled at just over 4½ miles (7.2 km) an hour, an impressive speed in those days.

The steamboat's success was an important achievement for Robert Fulton. When he first returned to America, many people doubted that he would be successful. They didn't believe that steam could actually be useful in water travel. In fact, before the vessel proved itself on the Hudson, it had often been jokingly called *Fulton's Folly*.

Frequently, Robert Fulton has been credited with the invention of the steamboat. However, this isn't true. In fact, over sixteen steamboats are

*Fulton's steamboat on its maiden voyage
up the Hudson passes delighted
onlookers at West Point.*

known to have been built in the United States before Fulton's. An American inventor named John Fitch built a steamboat nearly twenty years before Fulton returned to the United States. One of Fitch's steamboats actually sailed on the Delaware River as early as 1787. Fitch built two more steamboats within the next two years.

Fitch started a shuttle boat service to carry passengers between Philadelphia, Pennsylvania, and Trenton, New Jersey. However, he was never able to build a boat that traveled quickly enough to make it a desirable means of transportation. Therefore, there wasn't very much demand for his steamboating service and the business never prospered.

Meanwhile, other inventors had produced various types of steamboats. Often these vessels proved to have serious flaws. Some weren't capable of staying afloat. Others simply didn't travel at an acceptable speed.

So although Fulton didn't actually invent the steamboat, he produced the first commercially successful one. In fact, this talented inventor and able businessman had a great deal to do with making steamboats popular in America. Fulton took a personal interest in the comfort and safety of the passengers who boarded his steamboat. He oversaw the food's preparation in the vessel's galley. He

Left: This painting, entitled The First Steamboat, *shows one of Robert Fitch's early steamboats on water. Even though the boat had six paddles on its sides, it was still driven by steam engine.*

Below: Fulton's steamboat (later called the Clermont*) was first called the* North River Steamboat. *By 1807, regularly scheduled trips from New York City to Albany had been established.*

made certain that the meals were tasty and promptly served. He also insisted that the crew eagerly assist passengers and do all they could to make them comfortable.

While Fulton was involved in making the steamboat a success, he met Robert Livingston's second cousin Harriet Livingston. They fell in love and were married on January 7, 1808. Harriet not only bore four children, she did all she could to help and encourage her husband in his work.

Before long, Robert Fulton was able to take pride in the superior steamboat service he ran along New York's Hudson River. Within a few years, he had constructed two additional steamboats to navigate these waters. Fulton also designed a ferryboat that operated between New York and New Jersey. The ferry easily enabled out-of-state passengers to connect with Fulton's steamboats on the Hudson River.

Fulton and his financial partner, Robert Livingston, were encouraged by their success in New York. They decided to branch out. Fulton's steamboats had greatly improved travel conditions in the Northeast. The two men were convinced that steamboating might do well in other areas of the country too.

The men carefully studied maps and drawings

*Fulton's wife, Harriet Livingston, had come
from a wealthy family. However,
her parents had always stressed
the importance of spending money wisely
and enjoying life's simple pleasures.*

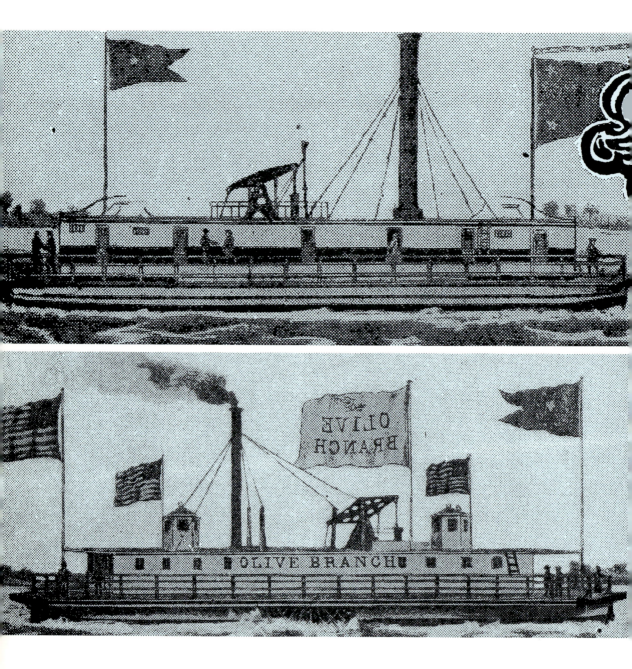

of both the Ohio and Mississippi rivers, as well as the areas surrounding these waterways. They petitioned the various states for the right to navigate their waters. Finally in 1811, Louisiana granted them the sole right to run steamboats along the Mississippi.

Robert Fulton designed a magnificent vessel for this purpose and named it the *New Orleans*. Built in Pittsburgh, Pennsylvania, Fulton's *New Orleans* was the first steamboat ever to travel on a river in America's interior. The attractive and efficient vessel enhanced both Fulton's fame and wealth. He continued to expand his work, and in time he ran over seventeen steamboats on America's waters.

During much of the time in which Fulton became successful, problems existed between En-

Fulton's ferryboats, shown here, carried passengers wishing to travel by water from New Jersey to New York City and back. However, Fulton's sole right to operate interstate boats on waters that bordered states involved him in numerous lawsuits with other businessmen who wished to do the same.

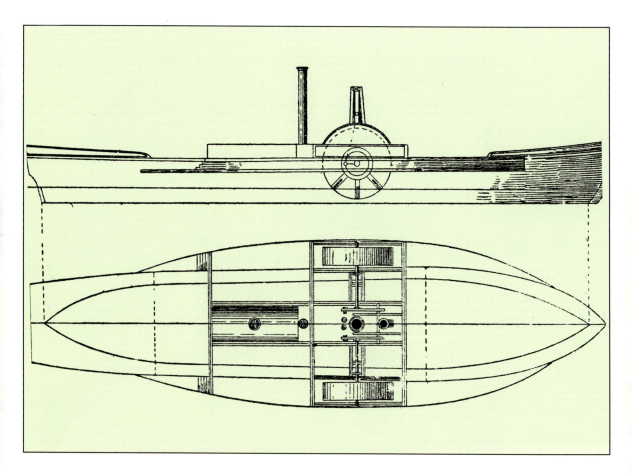

*Drawn after the **Clermont-North River**'s success,*
these plans for an advanced
steamboat include an improved engine.

Fulton's New Orleans, *pictured here,
was the first steamboat to travel the
Ohio and Mississippi rivers.*

gland and the United States. England interfered with America's overseas shipping. Some Americans also believed that the British had secretly encouraged Indian tribes to attack American pioneers heading westward. Tension between the two countries continued to mount, and before long the War of 1812 broke out.

Robert Fulton was prepared to do whatever he could to help his country. At the time, many New Yorkers feared that their city might be taken by the British. New York's eastern seacoast location made it an especially vulnerable target. The city needed a way to defend its harbor against an enemy attack.

Fulton designed a steam-operated war vessel to protect New York's harbor. Congress eagerly accepted his plans for the warship's design. The vessel, named *Fulton I*, was among the largest and most powerful warships ever built. But, unfortunately, Robert Fulton never saw it afloat on his country's waters. He became seriously ill and, in 1815, died at the age of forty-nine. At the time of his death, the ship was only partially constructed.

Robert Fulton was an exceptional man. He was much more than just a talented inventor and a resourceful businessman. Robert Fulton turned de-

Fulton I, *Robert Fulton's huge warship, was 156 feet long with a 16-foot paddlewheel.*

Estimate for the expence of a steam ferry boat
for one year

2 fire men at 30 dollars a month each they finding
themselves, they will also act as engineers to keep the
engine in order, they must be engaged for the year, as
such men cannot be turned away in the winter &
got in the Spring = 60 dollars a month —   720 a yeu

Two Boatmen to take turns in steering
at 25 dollars a month each 50 dollars   } — 600
a month — — — — — — — — — — — —

1 ½ Cords of wood for 12 or 13 hours at
4 ½ dollars a cord or say 7 dollars a day   } 2240
to work 320 days — — — — — — — —

Ware tare and Repairs — — — — — — — — — 600
                                   Total. 4,160

Robt Fulton
Jany 22d 1810

Estimate for the
expence of a steam
ferry boat for one
year

signs on paper into efficient vessels that connected many of America's waterways. He ushered steamboating into its own age of glory. Many people dream of doing great things. But Robert Fulton had the talent and determination to make dreams come true.

Robert Fulton was an able financial manager. This is a copy of his yearly budget for the operation of his ferryboats.

GLOSSARY

Apprentice—an individual who works for another in order to learn a trade

Device—something invented or built for a special use

Flax—a plant fiber used to make linen, thread, or woven fabrics

Hemp—the coarse fiber of a plant used to make rope or woven fabrics

Steam engine—an engine that operates through the power of steam

Vessel—a ship or boat

FOR FURTHER READING

Borja, Robert. *Steamboats to the West.* Chicago: Children's Press, 1980.

Gray, Michael. *Ships and Submarines.* New York: Franklin Watts, 1986.

Siegel, Beatrice. *The Steam Engine.* New York: Walker, 1986.

Stein, R. Conrad. *The Story of Mississippi Steamboats.* Chicago: Children's Press, 1987.

Williams, Brian. *Ships and other Seacraft.* New York: Franklin Watts, 1984.

INDEX

Boats: see *Ferryboats,*
  Steamboat, Submarines,
  Warships and ship
  names

Canals, 30, 32, 33, 41
Clermont (*North River
  Steamboat*), 42–43, 44,
  47

Delaware River, 45

England, 25–26, 32, 37,
  40–41

Ferryboats, 48, 51, 57
Fitch, John, 45, 47
France, 32
Fulton, Harriet Living-
  ston (wife), 48, 49
Fulton I, 54, 55
Fulton, Mary Smith
  (mother), 11, 12, 21
Fulton, Robert, Jr.
    as artist, 19, 22, 25–
      26, 27
    birth of, 11, 12
    boyhood experi-
      ments of, 15, 18

ABOUT THE AUTHOR

Elaine Landau received her BA degree from New York University in English and journalism and a master's degree in Library and Information Science from Pratt Institute in New York City.

Ms. Landau has worked as a newspaper reporter, an editor, and a youth services librarian. She has written many books and articles for young people. Ms. Landau lives in Sparta, New Jersey.

To: Bernie
From: Dallas Sigma Team

To share our goal for the year 2001 with you. We are going to our destiny to be a top performing sales team. (Top 10%). We are determined to fulfill our dream to be a team we can all be proud of.
We are going to help drive Sigma West to our winning position—#1. It will require perserverance and discipline on the fundamentals. Keep it simple and watch us soar.

Sincerely,
Ana Roland
'01

GO TO YOUR DESTINY

BY ALVIN AND CALVIN HARRISON

Foreword by André Farr

NEW YORK

Edited by Mark Vancil

Copyright © 2000 by Alvin and Calvin Harrison, Inc.

ISBN 0-7868-6788-4

First Edition
10 9 8 7 6 5 4 3 2 1

DEDICATION

We dedicate this book to Lucille Harrison and Emperor Haile Sellasie I, with the love of God's sons.

ACKNOWLEDGMENTS

We would like to first thank our Lord and Savior Jesus Christ from whom all of our strength and talent come. To our sister Africia, with our love and forever remembrance. Special acknowledgments to our parents, Albert and Juanita, our siblings and our families. Thank you all for your patience and support.

THANK YOU

Special thanks to Oprah Winfrey, a great friend and inspiration, Bob Miller and staff at Hyperion, Mark Vancil and staff at Rare Air Media and especially Davide Stennett for the very best photography.

Along the way there have been hundreds if not thousands of friends, fans and well-wishers that have prayed for us and supported us over the years. Thank you all from the bottom of our hearts. To our teammates, coaches, teachers and community leaders, thanks for all the work you put into us and the generous words of encouragement.

EXTRA-SPECIAL THANKS

Extra-special thanks to André Farr for being a friend and confidant and, most importantly, for your professional guidance. Extra-special acknowledgments to James Farr and Danielle Frost for your hours of dedicated work and commitment behind the scenes.

PHOTOGRAPHY CREDITS

AP/WIDE WORLD PHOTOS	14-15, 82-89, 91-96, 134
BRIAN BAHR, *Allsport Photos*	10-13, 16
CORBIS/BETTMAN	81, 129, 131, 135, 140-142, 144
HARRISON FAMILY COLLECTION	49-64
JED JACOBSOHN, *Allsport Photos*	11
SPORTS ILLUSTRATED	6-7, 130-134, 136-139, 142-143
DAVIDE STENNETT	1, 3
MATTHEW STOCKMAN, *Allsport Photos*	11

CONTENTS

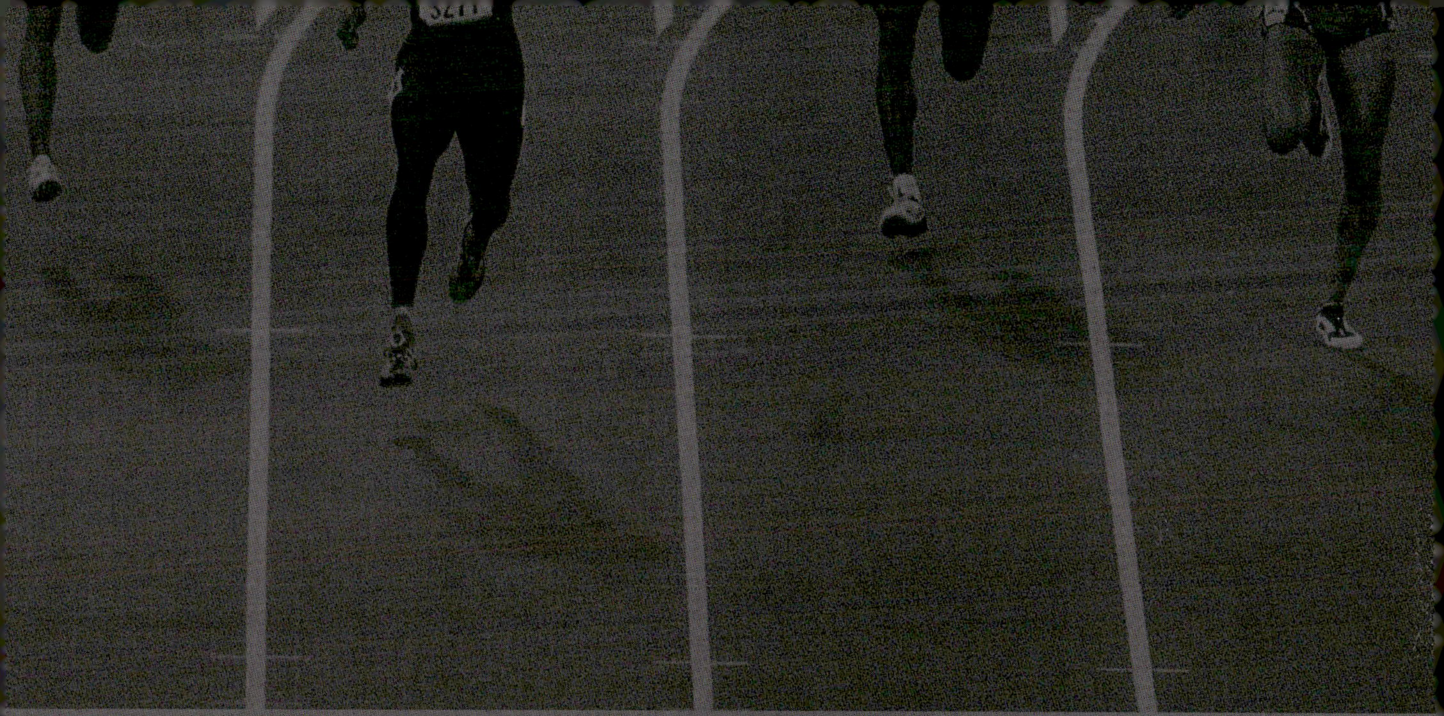

FOREWORD

Go to Your Destiny is not a book written in a traditional non-fiction format. It is a testimonial. A first hand account of two lives woven together by fate and held together by faith. Identical twins, Alvin and Calvin Harrison endured hard times, experienced life's unfairness, yet realized that their ultimate power to overcome adversities in their lives could be summed up in the simple phrase "Together we will."

What an honor it is to be allowed to write the Foreword for a book written by two incredible human beings. This is a story that is as much about humanity as it is about athletics. Young, innocent and naive as poor children from the South, Alvin and Calvin manifest themselves into top world-class athletes while they simultaneously learn the harsh

BY ANDRÉ FARR

realities of life on their own. The Harrison twins are a throwback to a simpler time when athletes were just people. The world should be exposed to the fascinating and heartwarming story of the "Twins".

To appreciate their story is easy, but to fully understand their story is a complex journey—a journey that most can't comprehend let alone endure. Theirs is a story of love, faith and the unrelenting will to fulfill promise.

Someone once said, "The true measure of a man's character can be found when severe adversity befalls him." Alvin and Calvin have both triumphed when the world believed otherwise. From poverty, abandonment and ridicule, these two have survived the unsurvivable, conquered the unconquerable, and have won the

unwinnable. Their story is the true embodiment of human will. Their undeniable belief in self, their ultimate trust in one another, as well as their unwavering conviction in the Lord Jesus Christ, have made them a true testament of faith to the world over.

Every so often there comes a person who shows the world something so awesome, so inspiring that words cannot describe the magnitude of that person's influence and inspiration. In Alvin and Calvin, the world has been granted two. Their humble spirit, innate wisdom and amiable personalities make them the perfect combination to touch lives and influence people to continue to strive in the face of despair.

Go to Your Destiny is a first-hand account of how two children, underprivileged in terms of material

wealth, discover that they are abundantly rich in spiritual necessities. They never made excuses. They never questioned their faith. They never quit. Their continued love for family and trust in fate against all odds make them a true inspiration.

I know that I am truly blessed to be able to call Alvin and Calvin friends. Although we share a professional relationship, they have accepted me as a big brother and a confidante. They inspire me more than they will ever know. I firmly believe we were brought together to do great things. I believe in them as much as I believe in their words. I encourage you to say to yourself, as I say to myself everyday, "Go to Your Destiny!"

Getting my game face on at the 2000 Olympic Trials in Sacramento. **CALVIN**

THIS WAS THE FIRST HEAT of the 400 meters at the 2000 Olympic Trials. At this level, shoes play a major role in making you feel comfortable. I wore these shoes for the first two rounds before switching to another pair for the semifinals and finals. I felt good that first day of the Trials. I'm just concentrating on advancing to the next round while conserving as much energy as possible. I want to run fast, but I'm more concerned with being ready for the next day. **ALVIN**

I'M CONCENTRATING ON MY RHYTHM

As soon as I'm out of the blocks I'm using every sense in my body to understand what's going on around me ... I'll process that information while I'm concentrating on my rhythm. **ALVIN**

MY MIND IS

GOING 100 MILES AN HOUR

Am I in the right position? Are my arms where they are supposed to be? Am I in rhythm? What are the other runners doing? Everything you can imagine is going through your head during the course of a race. **CALVIN**

We went to Australia a few weeks before the Sydney Olympics started just to maintain our conditioning and focus. Calvin (right) and I ran away with this race at Nudgee Stadium in Brisbane, Australia. These events are sometimes called 'testing meets' because you are trying to remain sharp without peaking too far in advance of the Games. I won this race in 44.74 and Calvin finished second in 45.07, both very good times. **ALVIN**

We're all smiles on our victory lap after qualifying for the 2000 United States Olympic Team in the 400 meters. Antonio Pettigrew (far left) finished third, Michael Johnson (second from left) finished first, Alvin finished second and I finished fifth. Jerome Young isn't in the picture, but he finished fourth. The top six in the 400-meter finals at the Olympic Trials qualified for the U.S. Team. **CALVIN**

CHAPTER ONE

GO TO YOUR DESTINY

CALVIN

We passed the night in the quiet and darkness of a hotel room near Hornet Stadium on the campus of Sacramento State University the same way we had passed thousands of other nights in our lives together. Alone with each other, Alvin and I talked a little after turning out the lights. Conversation, particularly at this point in our lives, really isn't necessary but the words broke the silence and provided a measure of comfort as we settled into our rest. They say identical twins share a unique bond that extends into the spiritual world. Ours is born of that world. I can't imagine a stronger bond between siblings than what Alvin and I share. The energy that passes between us is palpable. Though we are each other's counsel on almost everything, our feelings, fears, hopes and dreams most often are communicated on the wind between us. The connection is that strong, that deep. I can send Alvin energy, a positive vibe or a sense of security through the wind. I can feel the energy leaving me and Alvin can feel it coming into him. I even can feel the vibe the way Alvin is feeling it. So after a day of exorcising yet another demon, and with the anticipation of achieving a goal that might otherwise have seemed ridiculous to mention, much less entertain just a few years earlier, I knew exactly what Alvin was thinking as we settled into the beds amid the calm and quiet of our room. Alvin knew exactly what was rolling through my mind as well.

ALVIN

From the time we were old enough to understand what was happening, Calvin and I have had visions of events and experiences before they happened. When I was little the visions scared me. I wasn't sure what to make of them, particularly when I realized what I had seen in a vision actually was happening in real time. I remember being conscious of the regularity with which these glimpses of the future would come, and I was afraid that one day or night I would see myself die. These visions are so clear and come to pass so often that I knew seeing my own death would lead to its manifestation. Though I never have seen myself die, Calvin and I just assumed everyone had this ability, or gift. Sometimes we aren't able to make an immediate connection to what we might have seen in a dream or a vision. Other times, the actual event has a slight variation, but the same conclusion. When my little sister Africia was murdered in 1996, I saw it happen in a

vision, only I thought it was happening to my brother. In the vision, Calvin and I were running and I had hold of his right arm with my left hand. I could see the bullets – seven of them – coming toward him and I would jerk his arm one way or the other to make him avoid them. My sister was shot seven times just a few weeks after the 1996 Olympics.

CALVIN

We always have felt a bond with nature, the ground, the wind, the water. Sometimes the visions come to me at night, usually between 4 a.m. and 6:30 a.m. It's the same with Alvin. Other times, the visions come to me through wind or out of a tree. I always see them at an angle as if they are coming to me through the eyes of the wind. I know it sounds crazy, but the same bond Alvin and I feel with one another is the connection we feel to nature, to God. To us these visions and the way they come to us seem reasonable. We were raised by our grandmother, Lucille, who had a spiritual aura around her that just shined. From the minute she got up in the morning until she went to sleep at night, she would either be praying or humming hymns. Looking back, we feel like God used our grandmother as a conduit to help us understand these visions and the connection we have to nature. We had so many hands over us and so many people, usually a group of ladies who were friends of our grandmother, praying over us and praying for us that having a special gift or insight somehow seems reasonable to us. But as we lay in our beds the night before the 400-meter final in the 2000 Olympic Trials, the only pictures rolling through our minds were those created by us. Though we have had the ability to see things since as far back as we can remember, visual imaging techniques are something we had to learn. In the darkness of that room, Alvin and I were mentally running the race we would physically run the next day. We have trained our minds to utilize visual imaging just like we have trained our muscles to respond on the track. By going over the race in our minds we are trying to initiate the manifestation of those images. Even in the darkness, my heart began to pump as I saw the race unfold. Each of us knew our lane positions for the final and we knew every other runner in the field. I watched the race unfold from Lane 1, which is where I was positioned. Generally, Lane 1 and Lane 8 are the two worst spots to be on the track in a 400-meter race. In Lane 1, everyone is ahead of you. In Lane 8, everything is behind you. It's common to see the last two runners in a 400-meter race come from those two lanes. It's almost like information overload for a guy in the first lane versus a complete lack of information for the guy on the outside. Although I would have preferred to be elsewhere on the track, I couldn't introduce a negative into my thought process. I told myself the lane didn't matter. I had put the work in and I was ready. I ran the race over and over in my mind, and each time I saw myself winning. That's not easy to do when someone as dominant as Michael Johnson is in the race. But I beat him all night long.

ALVIN

There is the tendency to lose concentration and slowly begin to focus on the negative the night before a big race. You are lying there trying to relax, but you can feel your heart beating. I knew the hours were passing and I wasn't getting any sleep. But the mind is a very powerful tool. I knew that if I allowed myself to introduce that fact into my consciousness, then it could manifest itself on the track the next day. It was just sleep. Calvin and I had prepared ourselves for this moment. We had done everything necessary to achieve this objective, and a lack of sleep never would be enough to undo all that we had done. We were going to qualify for the 2000 United States Olympic Team. I had no doubt about that. By the time I reached the track there wouldn't be a man alive able to run faster than me.

CALVIN

For me, the semifinal race earlier in the day had taken on a life of its own. The day had set up in 2000 exactly as it had four years earlier. In 1996, Alvin ran in the first semifinal heat and qualified for the final. I was running the second. I needed to finish in the top four to move on and have a chance for the Atlanta team. But I was out of rhythm almost from the moment I got out of the blocks. Rhythm is the beat to which a runner moves through a race. It sounds like a simple process to stay to a one-two, one-two beat. But that rhythm has to become part of your soul, something you can feel down to the smallest movement. In 1996, I ran the first 100 meters in 11.2 seconds, which was way too slow. Then to catch up I ran a 9.8 my second 100 meters, which is way too fast for the 400 meters. Now I had to play catch up to get into position. By the last 100 meters my fuel tank was on empty. That's a lonely feeling. There was no one out on that track to help me but myself. The only thing I could do was hope and pray I had a little more strength to bring it home. I didn't. Jason Rouser and I crossed the line in a photo finish. We immediately turned around and looked up at the big screen. He won the fourth spot in the final by 7/1000ths of a second. I hurt more than I could have imagined. Alvin and I had turned our lives upside down at a time when neither of us knew what might happen next. A year earlier, in 1995, we had moved back to California from the Orlando ghetto where we had been raised. We had no money and nowhere to stay, but we jumped in an old Mustang and drove it across the country to Salinas, California, where we had lived with our father through high school. We spent weeks living in that car, flipping a coin to see which one of us would get the backseat (Alvin) and reading the Bible. No one believed it was possible for anyone, particularly Alvin and I because of our lives at that time, simply to make a decision to chase the 1996 Olympic Team. Though we had had our moments, I had run the fastest time in the 400 meters ever by a high school student just two years earlier; the idea of starting over with a singular goal of making the Olympics seemed crazy even to those closest to us. Then to get close, only to fail by the split of a second, was devastating. I felt cheated, like the whole world was against me. At the same time, I knew

Alvin had to compete the next day in the final. I had to focus on Alvin making it because one of us had to represent our family and everyone who had believed in us to that point. I did everything I could the next day to help him. I helped Luis, our trainer, stretch Alvin before the race. Alvin ended up finishing third behind Michael Johnson and Butch Reynolds, running a personal-best 44.09 that is still one of the 10 best times ever run in the 400 meters. What made Alvin's performance so amazing that day was the fact he had run – and won – his first 400-meter race against international competition just three months earlier.

So as the semifinals approached in 2000, I found myself dealing with the memory of what had happened in 1996.

ALVIN

I refused to leave the track after my semi-final race in 2000. I had to be there to see him run. I knew I could help Calvin around the track if I was there, so I stayed on the infield and focused on him. As Calvin got into the blocks the anticipation was building for me too. I'm saying to myself, "We trained hard enough to accomplish this feat. Do exactly what we have practiced." I'm sending out this vibe on the wind to Calvin. I'm looking at him. I'm completely focused on Calvin and I'm saying, "Run with my strength, run with my mind, run just like me." I'm just trying to manifest everything that we have done to prepare for this point, and I'm watching his every step. I noticed he got out of the blocks good. I think, "Great, just maintain. Stay in that position. Don't go any faster because you don't have to." After he finished the first 200 meters I'm thinking, "OK this is where the race starts." I kept trying to send my strength out to him and I'm saying, "Just run like me, run like me." He brought it home just the way I would have. I remember feeling like just half of me was standing there as I waited for the race to begin. When it was over, and Calvin had made the finals, I felt whole again.

CALVIN

As we walked over to the warm-up track ahead of the final, I watched people pass by but I really didn't see them. I saw the outline of the stadium and I could hear the crowd, but it was as if everything had the softness of a dream. Yet I could feel everything. I could feel the air, hear the wind, and everything seemed more vivid. Alvin and I slipped off our shoes and stood in our bare feet on the infield grass. We knew this was our time. We were in Northern California, which had become our home. Our ups and downs had played out in front of many of these people since high school in Salinas, just outside Monterey. Alvin and I had led our high school team to the California state track and field championship in 1993. We had no idea of the valleys that would follow that success, the sense of loss born of tragedy and the ghosts of our childhood. We had been counted out and left behind in the minds of coaches, competitors and virtually everyone else around us at one time or another. But on this day, in Sacramento, the warm sun felt like a blanket. Alvin and I removed our shoes to allow blood to move more efficiently through out feet. The grass slipped in between my toes, the ground felt soft, almost nurturing as I jogged around the infield of the practice track. Alvin and I talked about the race. We traded positive energy, reminding one another of all that we had done to prepare for this moment. Our destiny was right there in front of us.

A   L   V   I   N

Once you get to the track, the intensity is apparent. As much as you prepare for that moment, there is a small amount of anxiety just because you're human. You're nervous. Your heart is beating all day. You have to be aware of slowing down your heart rate to conserve as much energy as possible. You're thinking about getting out of the blocks those first 15 meters. You know you have to push early and then try to set yourself up for position. We had run against every guy in the race, and we knew their strengths and weaknesses.

Everything that had come before and everything that lay ahead would come together in these 400 meters. Our father, with whom we lived through high school after leaving Florida, was in the stands. There were all kinds of people from the scattered corners of the previous eight years there as well. Ed Barber, our high school coach, had a seat. So too did Gary Shaw, the coach Alvin and I had in our brief stop at Hartnell Community College. There were brothers and sisters, some half and some whole, and my father's wife, Frederica. I don't know if it was the pain still lingering somewhere inside or the harshness or their absence, but neither of us dwelled on the deaths of our sister, Africia, or our grandmother. They were there too, we knew, somewhere high above looking down and providing strength. Knowing our grandmother, she had her hands over our heads and was deep in prayer. Our little sister had been the one person who never wavered in her belief in our ability to win. At a time when all we wanted to hear from our father or mother were those words of support, the only person who consistently provided them was Africia. No one in the world, certainly no one in the world of track and field, thought we could beat Michael Johnson. Africia always told me she knew I could.

*   *   *

Great athletes have the ability to use all their senses all the time. The greatest athletes generally utilize their senses to the greatest degree. I think that's especially true in track and field. As the start of the race approaches, your senses slowly are becoming more tuned in to what you are about to do. Everything is heightened, from the grass between your toes to the thumping of your heart to the events running through your mind. There are three calls before a race and on the third call you have about 10 minutes to head over to a tent to check in and receive your numbers. That's when you start getting nervous. You're not scared, but there is no heading back. The time is approaching fast and everyone knows it. It's not like football where you get four downs. There's only one shot in track and field. No one is making eye contact. In fact, there isn't a sound.

You have a bag with your gear and your spikes are in your hands as you walk into the tent. The first thing you have to do is show the officials your shoes so they can measure your spikes. They can't be any longer than a quarter inch. Then they look through the bag to make sure you don't have any headphones. If you do, they get confiscated. That rule was put in after an athlete listening to music on his headphones was speared in the neck by a javelin. At that point, all the horses are in the stable. The other runners are there, but no one is talking to one another. One of the funniest things is that everyone is so quiet. You could hear a pin drop in there. Everyone has his game face on. You get your stickers and your numbers to put on your unitard (uniform). I'm getting ready to run and trying to play music in my head to relax. I'm trying to think about my daughter or my son, anything that can relax my mind. I don't want to get too distracted, though. It's a fine line between conserving energy and maintaining focus.

Calvin and I always hug one another in the call room. We just want to provide security to each other, while letting the other one know that everything is all right and just the way it's supposed to be. Now we come out of the tunnel and onto the track, and we know this is it. The crowd was our crowd. People are calling our names, all our coaches are there watching us. There are signs with our names. Just about everybody that had been a part of our journey was there. I was so pumped that I remember thinking that no one on this planet can beat me today. I'm ready to roll. Calvin and I had gifts for the fans – some shirts we had signed, some glasses, spikes – that we threw into the stands.

CALVIN

As we head out of the tent and onto the track we can hear the fans. We're waving, Alvin is pumping his fist against his heart, and at that moment you feel like there never has been a man on earth capable of running faster than you are about to run. The other runners are looking straight ahead. There is no eye contact and not a word is spoken between the others. As we approach the blocks, Alvin and I hug one last time. After that moment, we're on our own. When Alvin leaves I'm trying to hear music in my head to calm my mind. For me, sometimes I'll go with some hard core rap and then other times I'll listen to really slow love songs. It puts me somewhere else for those moments because you have to conserve your energy.

Once I'm on the track, though, everything goes away. I'm listening for the call to get into my blocks. Two or three years ago, I would get into the blocks and think about what my first moves would be. Not now. I have gone over this race so often and in such detail that I no longer have to think about my moves. I know what to do. So I listen to my body. At that point my heart really is pumping. The first command is "runners take your marks," and I take a deep breath and get down into position. The last command is "set." When I'm in the set position I don't hear anything. And I don't want to hear anything because I am completely tuned into hearing the gun.

ALVIN

When Calvin leaves for his blocks and I start walking over to mine, I know there is nothing more I can do for Calvin. And there is nothing Calvin can do for me. We always tell each other, "I'll see you at the top of the mountain." Now you are in your zone. Although we're running the race together and our goal is to finish first and second, at the same time it's like Calvin doesn't exist and in Calvin's mind I don't exist. It's a fine balance at that point. We respect one another and we love each other, but we each have our jobs to do.

We're just now starting to understand how to run the 400. It's a parallel to life really because people are always going to be pushing you and presenting challenges. But you can't run their race, or attack based on someone else's expectations for you. You have to maintain your own focus and go your own way at your own speed. You can't panic. You have to listen to yourself and follow your own destiny. I think a lot of our strength came from our grandmother.

She was a very strong woman. When she was a young girl she had to quit grammar school to pick cotton in Georgia to help her mother and father. Her father, Garfield, was blind so she had to help take care of her two sisters. And she worked hard like that her whole life. She took on washing clothes and cleaning houses to make money to buy the house we were raised in. She walked nearly 10 miles to and from work every day.

In fact, that's how she met my grandfather. He would be hanging around with some guys along her path every day, and they would see one another. My grandmother used to take a short cut through a field and one summer the bushes had grown so thick that she couldn't take that route any longer. My granddad grabbed a sling blade and cut a path for her, and that's how they first got together. My point is that you can see her inner determination, the strength inside that pushed her forward. That was the strength she gave the rest of the family, particularly Calvin and me. She was stronger than a lot of the men who were around when we were growing up, not just mentally and spiritually but physically.

C A L V I N

I'm confident, but I'm just absorbing the moment and listening for the gun. My heart is pounding. I know what I have to do. I just need to hear the gun to initiate the whole thing. If anything, I'm just thinking about two numbers – 1, 2, 1, 2. As soon as the gun sounds, Pow!, it's almost a relief because now I can control my destiny. This is my opportunity. Everything else that has come before has been leading to this opportunity. Now I'm here.

The first 10 meters I'm going big arms, which means I'm pumping my arms and using my upper body strength to drive out of the blocks. I know that if I get out of the blocks, then I'll be all right. The body produces ATP (adenosine triphosphate) from food and then ATP produces energy as needed by the body. You can either use your ATP or lose it in track and field. If you use it, then ATP can be an advantage because it can propel you out ahead of everyone else. If you don't use, you lose it. That's why I get out fast. It's the first source of energy your body uses, and it's crucial to your rhythm to burn it up early.

Once I get to 300 that's when the race really starts to get interesting. The staggers even out and everyone is pretty much even. At that point, all I'm trying to do is maintain the rhythm. If I'm able to do that then I'll be fine because you are not going to go any faster after 300 meters. When you pass guys over the final 100 meters, it's not because you are going faster. They simply are going slower because they could not maintain their speed.

A L V I N

As soon as I'm out of the blocks, I'm using every sense in my body to understand what's going on around me. My peripheral vision allows me to see the other runners and where they are. I'll process that information while I'm concentrating on my rhythm. Am I where I'm supposed to be? Am I in good shape relative to the guy two lanes over? I'm not looking at anyone, but I can see them. I'm listening to their feet. I can hear them breathe. I can even feel the guys behind me. It's as if my ears have become eyes behind my head. I can hear a guy break his rhythm by listening to his steps. It's just like that antelope being chased by a cheetah on the Serengeti Plain in Tanzania. Don't think for a second he doesn't hear every single step that cheetah's making. That's how it is for us. You hear and feel everything.

C A L V I N

My mind is going 100 miles per hour. Am I in the right position? Are my arms where they are supposed to be? Am I in rhythm? What are the other runners doing? Am I where I'm supposed to be at the top of the turn at 300 meters? Do I have enough energy left? Is my head in the right place? What about my neck and shoulders? Am I taking enough steps? Everything you can imagine is going through our heads during the course of a race. There are checkpoints every 15 to 20 meters and I'm processing all kinds of information with every one of my senses.

At the top of the turn I can hear the crowd, so I know Michael Johnson is making his move. I stay relaxed. At that point I'm also thinking about Calvin. Where's Calvin? Where's Calvin? We're coming down the homestretch. At about 350 meters I see someone on the inside that I think is Calvin, but it's Antonio Pettigrew. I cross the finish line behind Michael in second place and I turn around to look at the screen to see what happened to Calvin. I need to know. I go over and say, "How did you do?" He is looking at the screen too.

I knew I made it, but I didn't know where I finished. We all were looking up at the board and there it was, fifth place, with the top six going to Australia on the United States Olympic Team. Alvin and I hugged and someone threw an American flag down to us onto the track. We took a lap around the track with some of the other runners who made the team. I remember feeling this sense of relief combined with an overwhelming excitement. We had done what no one thought was possible. And we weren't through yet.

Later on that night I was thinking about the day, and I remembered something that happened to us in 1996 a few weeks before the Olympic Trials in Atlanta. Calvin and I were hiking outside of King City at a place called Arroyo Seco, a beautiful place with deep canyons and gorges with waterfalls and rivers running through them. It's a mountainous area about 40 minutes from our home in Salinas. I wanted to climb this one mountain in particular but we were following a river. It came to a point where the river continued through a very narrow spot. We couldn't cross because it was too steep. The wall looked like it had a little lip on top, so we thought we could just climb up and go around this narrow area and we would be fine. But once we started climbing we realized the wall was not at all as it appeared. There was nowhere to go but almost straight up. The terrain was so precarious that either one of us could easily have fallen to our death. Calvin went first, and as he put his hands and feet into these narrow little holds, the rock would crumble and fly down into my face. We were holding on to little pieces of rock just to keep moving. I would take one hand off the wall, and Calvin would use my hand to push off and keep going. Then I would reach up and grab his pants to pull myself up as he struggled to hang on. We quickly realized we couldn't go back down because the wall was too steep. Once we started climbing, the only place to go was up. There were jagged rocks and water down below so there was literally no place to go. We had to keep climbing. We were working together this whole time just trying to get ourselves up the incline. My foot was shaking so badly that I didn't know whether I could hold on. We didn't know what we had gotten into. The rocks were razor sharp and the higher we got the tougher it got. You did not want to look down. We felt like we were getting closer, but we also realized that anything could happen at any minute before we got to the top. We literally were facing our mortality at that moment. We couldn't go back to where we started. Going backward might kill us. We had to keep climbing that wall. And all the while we thought we knew what we would find when we reached the top.

We finally made it, and when we looked up there was nothing but lush green pastures. There were deer on one side and trees, wildflowers for as far as you could see. It wasn't until the night of that race in Sacramento that I understood the life lesson of that experience. We survived because we relied upon one another. I knew that if we were going to keep going forward toward our ultimate goals and objectives we would have to do it together. But I also knew that whatever challenges were ahead, they probably would be something other than what they appeared to be at first glance.

2

GIVE ME MY ROSES WHILE I'M STILL ABLE TO SMELL THEM

ALVIN

Our grandmother's bed was just inside the front door, to the left against the painted cinder block wall. The bed doubled as a chair during the day because the house was small relative to the number of people living there. The white sheets, blankets and pillowcases rested against the aqua-colored wall. A green rug covered the floor. I used to pick up that rug when I was little. In some spots, there was nothing between that rug and the ground. It wasn't until I was a little older that I realized the dirt I saw was the same dirt just outside the front door in the yard. My grandmother's father built the front part of the house and our grandfather, James Harrison, built the back half in the 1940s. The house sat on the corner of Lennox Boulevard and Aaron Avenue in a part of Orlando that was almost 100 percent African-American. While I would like to call the neighborhood something else, the fact is it was the ghetto. But that house was home to Calvin and me. Later on, neighborhood kids let us know that our house was at the low end of the standards even for the neighborhood. The house, our shoes and the way we dressed weren't much of an issue to us until we were old enough to go to school and become the targets of the innocent cruelty of children. We didn't have a lot, not much at all actually. But we had a grandmother whose presence made our world seem safe and comfortable. Inside those doors we grew up at the foot of our grandmother, Lucille. From as far back as we can remember, Calvin and I would wake up in the morning and head straight for Grandma's bed. She would swing her legs over the side and sit there watching television. Calvin would sit down next to her left leg, and I would take my place next to her right leg. We would hold on to those legs all day and into the night. If we had to go to the bathroom, we would leave and come right back to that spot. Even at dinner, we would grab our food and carry it back to be next to her. She was more than the light of our lives. She was, even according to our biological mother, our real mother. She had beautiful silver-gray hair and soft features. There was a warmth to her face, and she had these inviting eyes. There was something in those eyes that made you feel like everything was OK even amid the chaos of our childhood. If something needed to be corrected, you could see it in those eyes. Her skin was soft and brown. And she had a spiritual aura around her that you could actually see. There was something divine about her, and that much was clear to anyone fortunate

enough to be around her. From the day we were born she took Calvin and me as her own. Our mother was just 16 with one child already when we were born. She probably would have had a hard time taking care of one more, much less two at the same time. It wasn't like my grandmother took hold of us to help our mother, who was her daughter. She took us as her own, and that's the way it was around the house for Calvin and me. She seemed to see something in us that would take years of struggle before we could see it ourselves. All five of her children lived in the house when we were born. The neighborhood was rough and dangerous thanks in part to our uncles. If you wanted to walk on Lennox Boulevard you came to our house to ask permission. That's how violent these cats were. All of them had mean dispositions and aggressive personalities. They were nice to us because we were family and we were kids. To some extent we knew their presence provided a certain element of protection, particularly as we got older and better understood the dangers of our neighborhood. But we knew early on, and our grandmother seemed to know, that we were different from the other children. Most kids growing up in that environment had to be aggressive and physically tough. Calvin and I were always calmer. I don't know how much of that came from our grandmother and how much of that we were born with, but I do know we were rarely far from her side. She was the authority figure in the house. She was a strong woman, stronger than some of the men. She had this tremendous will and determination that only later we realized she had instilled in us. As Calvin and I got older, Grandma's knees would swell up to the point she could barely stand. There wasn't anything we didn't do or try to do for her. But I don't think we could have done anything that would have provided her with as much as she gave us.

C A L V I N

To this day, I never have felt more joy from doing anything than I did doing something to please my grandmother. If I could make her happy or bring pleasure to her day, then my day was complete. Alvin and I would do all kinds of things for her. Later on, after she had a stroke, her left arm didn't work, so we would massage that shoulder for her while she watched television. She loved it because it felt so good. We would move the shoulder up and down just like a massage therapist would do. It wasn't like we knew what we were doing. No one showed us and there certainly wasn't anybody getting massages in our house. I remember taking great pride in making her feel better. Alvin and I felt like we were her doctors because we were taking care of Grandma. Another time, Alvin and I fixed up the bathroom for her when we were 9 or 10 years old. The bathroom walls had the wood frames you see before they are covered. In our house, the frame was up against the cinder block. There was no dry wall or paneling to hide the cinder block or the pipes. Alvin and I found some paneling in the backyard that our uncles had brought home. They had good intentions, but they never really got around to fixing much. So we took that paneling, grabbed some nails and a hammer, and fixed up the bathroom. It stayed that way until the house was torn down in 1999. We also used to cook for her because she couldn't stand on her knees very long. And at least twice a week we would go to the rose bushes in the front of the house and pick roses for her. She always used to tell us, "Give me my roses while I'm still able to smell them." And that's what we did.

ALVIN

She would pray from morning to night, day in and day out. If she wasn't praying, you would hear this sweet humming coming from her. And she prayed for us constantly. Calvin and I had hands over us all the time growing up. Sometimes we would wake up and she would be standing there praying over us. Other times there would be all these ladies, our grandmother's friends, praying over us. That happened all the time. If we happened to wake up and walk out into the living room during Bible study, all the ladies would stop and start to pray over us. Looking back, it seems like we were experiencing God in a tangible form through our grandmother. She made us feel special, different from everyone else. In some ways, I guess we were. In fact, it wasn't until recently that Calvin and I realized hardly anyone else sees what we see, or feels what we can feel. Part of it comes from this connection with nature we have always felt. It

seems to have been born out of the connection with God that our grandmother introduced to us.

Now I know this might sound crazy, but we learned we could control the wind when we were children. Actually, it's not so much controlling the wind as playing with wind. That's really what we were doing. We would be outside, and one of us would tell the wind to blow and it would blow. I remember Calvin and I being in a field of tall grasses and asking the wind to blow. It was as natural a thing to do as climbing a tree or blinking an eye. We could do it and we just assumed it was something everyone could do. The louder we asked the wind to blow, the harder it would blow. A couple years ago we told Calvin's wife, Sasha, what we could do and, of course, she didn't believe us. We were having lunch at a Wendy's at the time so we took her outside and asked the wind to blow. And it did. She was shocked. Then we did it again another time, and she realized we weren't crazy. It's not like we can control the wind to affect a race or anything like that. It's simply a matter of being one with nature. That's something we have felt for as far back as we can remember. It's a connection that has always been real for us. In some ways I guess it's hard to understand why everyone doesn't feel a connection to the earth, wind and water as deeply as we do, especially given where we grew up.

C A L V I N

It was like we had this power but no one told us it was a unique gift. We were just playing with the wind the way kids play with dirt, gather leaves or roll around in the grass. The wind was just another one of nature's elements there to provide pleasure. It was as natural to us as running around the block or walking down the street. We had this extraordinarily spiritual person in our grandmother around us all the time, and we were children who didn't know any better. It seemed reasonable that we would be able to control the wind. But it wasn't just the wind. Alvin and I always have had visions of future events. For example, I had always been able to see what the day was going to look like before the day actually started. I just figured it was God giving me a picture of that day before I woke up. And it always looked exactly the way I saw it. It happens to this day. I see all kinds of things before they happen. I saw my son before he was born. I saw exactly what he looked like. And when he was born, it was him to a tee. Every detail of his face and his body was consistent with the vision of him I had seen. It really was as if I had seen him before. Most of the time it happens when I'm asleep but sometimes it happens when I'm lying down resting or meditating.

A L V I N

Sometimes I'll wake up from having a vision, and it scares me. Other times, particularly as I've come to realize not everyone shares these experiences, it makes me question what our real purpose is in this life. I think track is one thing we are supposed to do. Then I start thinking, "Has the Lord given us these abilities just to use them for success in track and field?" We know we're here to do some kind of work. And we know we have a special relationship with God and nature. It's like our grandmother was the conduit between our lives and the spiritual world. But we also feel a higher responsibility because of these gifts.

These are things we have never told anyone before, because we realized not everyone believes, like us, that these things are possible. I used to be self conscious about some of these experiences because I didn't want to try to convince anyone. But it's real and it's part of our lives. I'm at a place in my life where I don't care what everybody else thinks. I know.

CALVIN

This ability never really freaked us out because we just figured everyone could do it. Even now, I have these visions all the time of events in the future. It wasn't until recently that we even realized that we were doing something special. The majority of the time I'm not able to figure out what the visions mean at the moment. It's not until later, when the situation presents itself, that I think back and remember the vision.

As soon as we were old enough to understand, our mother told us this story about our birth. I'm not sure why she felt so compelled to tell us about what happened. Maybe she thought the story would make us feel an even stronger bond. But she said Alvin and I were premature when we were born. Alvin came first, I came two minutes later. By the time I came out Alvin had stopped breathing. The doctors actually told my mother he was dead. At that moment I let out this ear-piercing scream. It was the kind of scream that shouldn't have come from a premature newborn baby, and our mother said everyone in the room took notice. All of a sudden, Alvin started breathing again.

ALVIN

The breath of life was given back to me by my brother. From what our mother says, it seemed like the scream was a call to God. We were so young, and there is such an innocence and purity at birth, particularly between identical twins. Calvin seemed to feel the loss and he let out this cry to God, who restored life. My father wasn't there at the hospital. But when he received the call that we were born, he said he went outside and looked into the sky. It was late at night, and he said he saw two shooting stars passing through the sky. I don't know what these stories mean, but we heard them when we were very young. Our mother made a point to tell them to us.

*   *   *

Our grandmother also had all these home remedies, the kind you have to have if you wanted to survive the kind of childhood she endured. I remember reaching down to pick up some dirty clothes that were lying on a broken mirror. I just scooped my hand down there, and my right index finger caught the corner of that mirror. The cut was at an angle so deep that you could see the bone. The skin just peeled back. My grandmother took my hand and told Calvin and everybody else to go around the house and collect all the spiderwebs. She rolled all the spiderwebs into this little ball and placed it on the wound. She pulled the skin back over the spiderwebs. She did the same thing when Calvin nearly cut off his toe on that same mirror. He was running in his bare feet and his little toe caught the broken glass. That toe was nearly cut completely off. My grandmother collected the spiderwebs and put them on the hole between his toes and bandaged it up. It was so bad that if it happened today, Calvin would probably need surgery to put the toe back on. But the spiderwebs worked just like they worked on my finger. She also used syrup to heal burns. Our grandfather used to have one cup of coffee every morning. He would take the cup off the saucer and place it right on the edge of the table. He knew Calvin and I loved to finish his coffee. He'd leave just enough to cover the bottom of the cup, and we would come by and drink what remained. One day the cup was sitting on the edge of the table full of steaming hot coffee. Calvin reached up and this hot coffee spilled all over the left side of his face. His skin went white from the burn. My grandmother put syrup on his face every day for a week, and the color of his skin came back. You couldn't even tell he had been burned.

C A L V I N

The house we grew up in was right in the middle of the lot on about a quarter acre. There were fruit trees in the back – banana, grapefruit, orange – and a pecan tree. There also was this huge chinaberry tree. That tree was our refuge. If something was wrong we would climb high into the tree. We knew every branch. We would eat whatever we had brought with us and just play around by ourselves away from everything and everyone else. If somebody wanted to mess with us, they were going to have a heck of a time trying to reach us. We spent most of our play-time in that tree. There was a garden that was to the rear of the house and a little storage-like shack in the back, too, where our grand-mother's sister lived for a while. We used to climb up on the roof and jump off. We would do that all day long. Maybe the strangest thing we did was run around the block every morning. We would get out of bed in the morning, put on our shoes and run around the entire block. It must have been 500 to 600 meters. We would do that every day and then just come back in the house. I don't know why we did that, but we did. Otherwise, the neighborhood was what you might expect in a poor part of the South. There was a lake not far away behind some houses and you would see guys going fishing with cane poles. There were guys hanging out on the corners, kids running around.

Our mother, Juanita, was 14 when she had our older sister, LaSandra. She and my father lived together in an apartment in Orlando after LaSandra was born. By the time we came along a couple years later, they had moved into my grandmother's house on Lennox Boulevard. My father was 10 or 11 years older than my mother, but they were still together until Calvin and I were 3 or 4 years old. They had another baby, my little sister Africia, and then broke up. For most of the early years of our childhood neither one of them was around much. My mom had three kids and was only 16 or 17, and she probably felt like she was missing out on life. I'm sure she had friends who didn't have kids who were partying and having the time of their life – things she wanted to do, too. I'm also sure she went out and did those things, which is why we were left with our grand-mother. By the time we were 5, our father was living on the other side of town, trying to carve out a life for himself. It wasn't uncommon or uncomfortable for Calvin and me to be at home alone with Grandma. For most of our early years she was our father and mother.

Our dad spent a lot of time trying to establish a life for himself after he and our mother split up. He would stay in touch, and we would talk to him every couple weeks. It wasn't like he abandoned us or anything like that. We knew we had a father and we knew he loved us. Looking back, I can see what he was doing and how difficult it was for him. Our mother was the one who tried to keep us away from him as we grew older. It was a control issue for her. Maybe she wanted to still be with him, and this was her way of trying to hurt him. A lot of parents use the kids in those kinds of wars and our situation was no different. I don't know what caused them to break up in the first place, but I do know that our father needed time to establish himself. He was a black man in the South in the late 1970s without a college degree. He had gone to community college, but he didn't have a four-year degree he could put to work. I'm sure there weren't a lot of high-paying jobs available to him. He would work construction jobs and sometimes live with our other grandmother, Josephine, who was his mother. What we didn't know at the time was that he was trying to create an environment that was much better than the one we were living in.

From the outside looking in there probably was plenty of reason to be scared in that neighborhood. Our ghetto was no different than the others in any city. But the only fear I remember having was the fear that came from being embarrassed. To get to our school, which was predominantly African-American, most kids had to walk past our house. The house was home to us, but it was a long way from being the kind of place you take pride in. The floors were that old kind of cement with rocks in it, the walls were cinder block and the ceiling wasn't finished. The cinder block walls were painted, but there wasn't much else in the way of decorating. We always wanted to be either the first kids walking to school or the last ones, because we didn't want to walk out of that house when a big pack of kids were coming by. Children can be very cruel. They just say what's on their minds with no filter. They would look at us and laugh. They would pick on us for the way we dressed, the shoes we wore, the house we lived in. They didn't have any mercy. If we feared anything it was the embarrassment that came with what other kids were saying about us.

Just riding around in a car was a luxury because our mom didn't have a car until we were older. One day she got an old Cutlass Supreme, and we were so excited. We couldn't wait to get inside and go for a ride. Calvin and I jumped into the back and we headed off to McDonald's. Riding in a car and going to McDonald's; that was a month's worth of fun for us. She didn't have the car that long, but she had it long enough for us to tell everyone at school our mother had a car. No one had much, so the focus was always on what you did have. Kids would talk about the new shoes they got, or the new jeans with the designer label. We didn't have any of those things, so they would pick at us, especially when we made someone angry. Calvin and I never wanted to make anyone upset or draw attention to ourselves because they would start picking at our clothes, our shoes, the house we lived in. I remember this girl, Louise, and she broke my heart. I was in love with this girl, that kind of puppy love you feel in seventh or eighth grade. I had this huge crush on her and I always was trying to make an impression. One day we were walking to the front of the class to put our papers on the

teacher's desk. I was coming from one side and she was coming from the other direction. I put my paper down and I continued to walk toward the bathroom. I bumped into Louise and her papers fell all over the floor. She told me to get my dirty butt away from her. I was devastated. What she said was true, which is what made it hurt so much. My clothes were dirty and I was wearing a pair of my uncle's old shoes, which were two sizes too big and worn out. I can talk about it now, but my heart was torn to pieces at the time. I had been trying to do little things for weeks to get her attention. Then she said that, and I realized what she really thought of me. We knew how we dressed, but at that age you think no one else notices if they aren't saying anything. She let me know that everyone was paying attention, and it was like a knife in the heart. Then, that same year, I went to a dance wearing a pair of my uncle's dress shoes. I didn't read the memo that said no hard shoes were allowed because the dance was on the gym floor. This time I had a girlfriend, and she was standing inside the dance waiting for me. They wouldn't let me in and sent me home to change my shoes. Now this was at Carver

Middle School, which was about 400 meters from our house. The principal and teachers at Carver were hard on you because of the area. The kids were rough and tough to the point they were actually fighting the teachers in the classrooms. So I went back home and changed shoes. I was so embarrassed, but I went back to the dance and danced with my girlfriend. We had a good time and I remember getting a kiss at the end of the night.

C A L V I N

This was the ghetto and the kids in our neighborhood were really rough around the edges. They were aggressive and most of them weren't afraid of fighting anyone, including the teachers. There was a big kid named Thadeous, who was supposed to be in high school but he was still in the seventh grade. He got into a fight with one of the coaches, Mr. Bingham. Mr. Bingham looked just like a little older Martin Lawrence. Thadeous looked like a light-skinned Ice Cube, he was that big. We were in gym class and Mr. Bingham was demonstrating wrestling techniques. Thadeous didn't want to participate because he didn't think

Mr. Bingham was showing the proper technique. They were going back and forth. Now teachers and students were used to saying things to one another that you wouldn't believe. Finally, the two squared off and Thadeous punched Mr. Bingham in the face. We were used to a rough environment, but we were astonished. Thadeous was bigger than the teacher and Mr. Bingham was staggering. Another teacher came along to break up the fight and we all headed into the locker room, where it started again. This time Thadeous took a brush and whacked Mr. Bingham in the back of the head. It was unbelievable but that kind of thing happened all the time.

A L V I N

One day this other kid got called to the principal's office for something he had done. He was a bad kid, more like a bully. Whatever he had done, Mr. Bradley, the principal, was giving this kid the paddle. Mr. Bradley hit him three times with that paddle. When he finished, this kid turned around, grabbed the paddle and slammed it across the principal's face. Keep in mind, this was junior high. We had to have a full-time policeman,

Mr. Albert, on campus at all times. Calvin and I never really had any problems because we were nobody then. We were real thin and kind of small so no one really thought of starting anything with us. But there was one time when I thought I would have to fight this big guy named Cornelius. He was another guy who should have been in high school, but he had been held back a couple times. He went to school about every other day. My little sister, Africia, had been in a fight with Cornelius's cousin. Africia was tough and she had beaten up the other girl. Well, Cornelius let everyone know that after school the next day he was going to whip Africia. So the bell rings and everyone starts walking out of the front gate. We get about 600 meters down the street and the crowd starts forming because everyone wants to see a fight. This guy is walking toward my sister, telling her he's going to beat her up. Now my little sister is rough and she gives it right back to him. He starts moving closer to her and now I'm called out. You have hundreds of students standing around and I have to jump in. I'm telling him, "I'm her brother, man, and you're not going to hit my sister." This guy doesn't care who I am because

he figures he will whip me too. Then out of nowhere comes this big guy we called Fat Albert. I had played on the football team with him just once, but he cuts through the crowd and tells Cornelius to back down. It's almost like God sent this guy. Cornelius just pops Fat Albert and knocks him backward. But Fat Albert comes back and unleashes a beating on Cornelius. The third time Fat Albert hits him, Cornelius flies over three bikes into a ditch. Mr. Albert, the policeman, comes running down the street, and Cornelius and Fat Albert end up in the backseat of Mr. Albert's car on the way to juvenile hall.

C A L V I N

As we got older and became more aware of what we didn't have and where we lived, I think we started worrying too much about what other people thought of us instead of what we thought of ourselves. I know it affected my self image. I remember wondering how I should act or how I should be. We were constantly looking around for clues because we didn't know. There wasn't a positive male figure in our lives as kids because our father wasn't around much. Our grandmother was our father, mother and spiritual guide. For the most part that was enough. Even with the stress of being embarrassed by your peers, whenever Alvin and I came home we found comfort with our grandmother. She was still able to make everything seem fine, which is incredible given what we were going through outside the doors of that house.

ALVIN

Calvin and I always have been more than brothers. We were each other's best friend and playmate. We went to the same schools, ate our lunch together, walked to and from school together. If something was bothering one of us, we would tell the other. If we were bothered by what other kids were saying or troubled by something, we would climb up into that chinaberry tree and spend all day together. We were each other's companion. It always has been that way and it's still that way today. Still, by the time sixth grade came around we were on the edge of adolescence, and we felt a need to be with our father. I remember being so excited about his phone calls. It's like we were growing up and we needed that connection to an adult male.

CALVIN

After we returned from Sydney in October of 2000, I started writing about different periods in our lives. This is what I wrote about the changes that were occurring in the summer before eighth grade:

It was early Friday morning and the phone rang. Our grandmother picked up the receiver and said, "Hey, Albert how you doing?" Realizing our father was on the other end of the line, we jumped up and down as happy kids do and shouted, "Grandma, that's Daddy. Can we talk to him?" I remember Alvin and I jumping, dancing on one leg, spinning around and just plain feeling happy about the chance to speak with our father. Our grandmother and father spoke for about 15 minutes before we got on the phone. Ecstatic to get the phone, we belted out "Hey Daddy, how you doing? We miss you. You going to send for us?" We were at a point in our lives that we longed to be with him. We needed the kind of security, love and friendship that only can come from your father. Our grandmother understood because we were about to be teenage boys. She had shared all the wisdom and love she could. She had done a fine job of raising us by teaching us all the basics: respect your elders, don't speak until you are spoken to, say yes sir and no sir. The good old Southern manners she had been raised with had been passed on to Alvin and me. But she knew we needed our father. And our father's reply was a dream come true:

"Yes, I am sending for y'all to come here to California. Do you guys want to come?"

"Yes, sir," we yelled.

"OK," he said, "your tickets will be ready in a couple days. I love y'all."

"OK, Daddy. We love you too."

We hung up the phone and raced to tell Grandma the news, which of course she already knew. But she listened attentively about our going to California.

After the excitement wore off, Grandma sat Alvin and me down and told us how we should act once we reached California. She sat slumped over in her daybed with her arms crossed rocking back and forth. She looked at us as she always did and said, "You my who?" I would smile and say, "Calvin." Then she would look at Alvin and say, "You my who?" And Alvin would smile and answer, "Alvin." Grandma would smile and shake her head up and down. She would end these exchanges with a "kiss on the hickey"

(forehead). And we did the same to her. It was our special kiss for one another.

Grandma proceeded to tell us to pay close attention to our father's rules. She told us to learn as much as we could at our new school and not to talk back to our father. Above all, she said, "Be respectful, honest and act like you have good sense."

Days passed and the more they did the closer we got to our departure. Alvin and I had rarely been out of the neighborhood, much less the city of Orlando. Even though we were happy to be going to live with our father, a part of us wanted to stay behind with the woman who had become our mother, father, caretaker, provider and shelter. Our grandmother was the one person we were attached to like no one else. We were connected not just emotionally, but spiritually. She was the person who had taught us about values and provided comfort and care during the hard times of childhood. I started to feel guilty and the closer the day came the more my mind raced with different questions. Who would protect Grandma? Who would go to the corner store when she needed something? Who would open the windows when she got hot or cover her with a blanket when she got cold? If I stayed, she *would have none of these worries because Alvin and I knew everything that needed to be done around the house. All of a sudden, moving to California didn't sound so great. I knew I would miss sitting on the floor next to my grandmother with my arms around her leg. I felt comfort and safety when I was in that position. So did Alvin, who sat on the other side. This great woman, who I believed to be an angel sent to us by God Himself, represented everything I knew to be good about life. I loved her so dearly that I wished and prayed she could walk on to the airplane with Alvin and me and experience all that we were going to see, eat what we were going to eat, and sleep where we were going to sleep. Oh, how I wanted her to grow old with us.*

Eventually, reality set in. For one thing, Grandma wasn't so kind about flying in airplanes. Secondly, there was no way Grandma would consider moving away from that house. It was home to her. I soon realized Grandma wasn't coming with us. And I knew I had some growing up to do. She had prepared us well, and now we were on our way to Salinas, California. We hugged and kissed and cried on the day we left for the airport. Grandma kept saying, "Be good now, and mind what your father tells you.

Y'all be good and don't be worrying about me, child. I'll be all right." Our aunt Ann came by the house and picked us up. We were about to see what else was out there.

The flight attendants were very kind to Alvin and me. I remember them bringing us as much juice and as many snacks as we wanted. This was the beginning of a great adventure, but all I thought about was how Grandma wouldn't see everything we would see. How could I not worry? I was so used to her being around, knowing that she was always there. The thought of being without her made me sick, literally. I felt depressed and guilty, and I cried. I cried some more when the plane landed in San Jose. Although I regained my composure and tried to look happy for my father, I couldn't get my grandmother out of my mind.

I remember the night air being cool, much cooler than Orlando. The sky was clear, stars were shining, and we were beginning to feel great. The ride to Salinas lasted about an hour. I used every minute to soak up the images of this new place. I stared at the mountains, the outlines of the trees against the sky, the signs directing us toward Salinas. I paid attention to just about every detail that surrounded me. I never had seen such great natural beauty. I remember looking at the mountains and the word "freedom" coming into my mind. The open fields looked like they went on forever without a beginning or an end. I felt an instant connection to the surroundings, as if they were telling me I could roll in the grass, climb the mountains, picnic on the beaches. Before long we pulled into the Bonnie Doone apartment complex on the east side of Salinas on North Madeira Street. Our father and his wife, Frederica, lived in apartment No. 1 with Frederica's two young sons. For the first time, Alvin and I would have our own room. This was the summer of 1989.

Our image of California was that we would see Tina Turner driving around in a limo. We had never seen hills in Orlando, much less mountains. Everything looked so different, so foreign. But living in that apartment was as stable as anything we ever had known to that point. I remember how everything seemed cleaner compared to where we had lived in Orlando. Calvin and I played on the asphalt parking lot and climbed a tree right outside the sliding door of the apartment. It wasn't nearly as big as the one behind my grandmother's house, but we hung out in that tree a lot. Calvin and I shared a bedroom, but it felt like we had our own room. Until that time, we had shared a twin bed since we were old enough to be out of the crib. Our mother and two sisters also slept in the same room with Calvin and me. There were hills in the back of the complex we would run up and down. My father got us a BB gun, and we would go into those hills and shoot at tin cans. We were just doing the things that kids did. I didn't realize how sheltered we had been growing up until we went to California. For most of our life everything was as simple as black and white. All our friends were black, the schools we attended were almost 100 percent black, and we never really played with anybody who wasn't black. In Salinas, the demographic was predominantly Mexican-American. At first, I couldn't tell the difference between a Chinese person, a Mexican or a Filipino. We grew up in a very closed environment. I was so ignorant about the rest of the world that I actually thought all Mexicans lived only in Mexico. I just couldn't tell one person from another. Everything was so different from what I knew.

C A L V I N

I saw the experience as more of an adventure. For two kids who considered a ride in a car and McDonald's the lap of luxury, California seemed like another planet.

Alvin and I went back and forth trying to identify ourselves in this photograph. I think that's me on the left with Alvin on the right. **CALVIN**

FROM THE DAY...

...WE WERE BORN, OUR GRANDMOTHER, Lucille, took Calvin and me as her own. We knew early on, and our grandmother seemed to know, that we were different from the other children . . . Calvin and I always seemed calmer. **ALVIN**

LOOKS LIKE

LEFT
We had just come home from the noon service at the Macedonia Baptist Church in Eatonville. This was during the time we were living with my father. Every Sunday after church we would go back to his apartment and swim in the complex's pool. **CALVIN**

RIGHT
Looks like another day after church. Our father lived in Altamont Springs, Florida, at the time. Alvin (left) and I are standing outside our dad's apartment with our step-sister, Stacey. **CALVIN**

NOTHER DAY AFTER CHURCH

LEFT
WE MUST HAVE just come home from church in Eatonville, Florida. We're standing in front of our dad's van at his mother's (Josephine's) house. The tallest one is our step-brother, Andre. Alvin is on the left and I am on the right with our cousin, Eric, whom we called Boo Boo, in the middle. The house sat on the corner of Campus View Drive and Hungerford Avenue, which is where all the drug dealers hung out. **CALVIN**

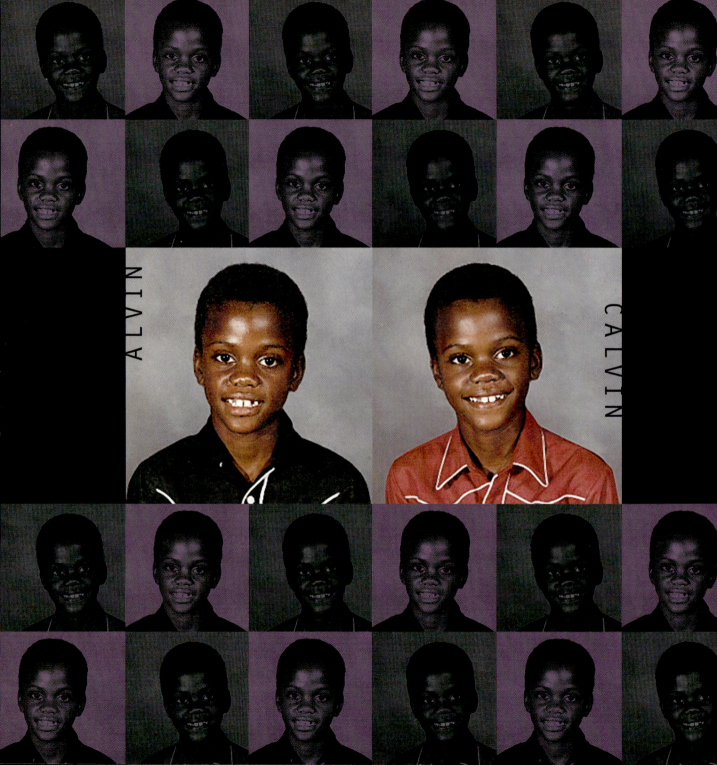
ALVIN

CALVIN

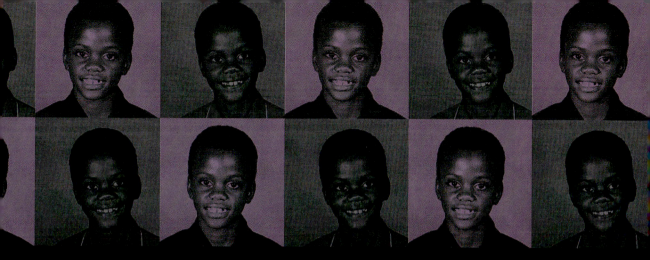

ALVIN AND I were always more than brothers. We were each other's best friend and playmate. We went to the same schools, ate our lunch together, walked to and from school together...We were each other's companion. **CALVIN**

AS WE GOT OLDER...

...AND BECAME MORE AWARE of what we didn't have and where we lived, I think we started worrying too much about what other people thought of us instead of what we thought about ourselves. **CALVIN**

RIGHT
Calvin (right) and I stand outside our
grandmother Josephine's house next to
our father's van on Easter Sunday. **ALVIN**

IT WASN'T LIKE I WAS GOING TO

WHEN I WENT TO CALIFORNIA for my eighth grade year, music was a much more logical focus for me because my father was a musician on the side. I'd play the keyboards and he bought me a drum machine to play with. It was around that time that I started writing songs. I wrote love songs primarily and a few rap songs. It wasn't like I was going to be a superstar or anything, but I liked the process. **CALVIN**

RIGHT
Until we moved to California at age 12, the only time we left Orlando was to visit our stepmother Fredrica's parents near Valdosta, Georgia. Here we are playing behind their house with our older sister, LaSandra. That's Calvin on the left. **ALVIN**

BE A SUPERSTAR OR ANYTHING

Our dad always had these cowboy hats so I grabbed his hat for this picture. It looks like I'm resting the radio on little Antonio's head. Alvin is standing with our other

56 | 57

THIS WAS THE KING CITY Invitational during our senior year at North Salinas High School. I can tell by the color of the track in the above photo. Calvin broke Steve Lewis's meet record in the 400 meters, which was a big deal because Lewis was one of the greatest athletes to come out of Northern California. He went to the 1988 Olympics right after high school. The photo on the left is Calvin (right) and me getting out of the blocks in the 200 meters. Calvin won the race and I finished second. **ALVIN**

ABOVE

Alvin (left) and me hanging out at the Bonnie Doone apartment complex in Salinas, California. Alvin had a piece of cartilage stuck under his knee cap, which is why he was wearing the walking cast. He never did have surgery to repair the problem. **CALVIN**

ABOVE

I had the nice fade going as a high school sophomore. I was heading off to Mrs. Loe's fashion show. **ALVIN**

ABOVE

Alvin (right) and I performed as a rap group at the Fort Ord Carnival in the summer before our junior year in high school. We went under the name "Double Vision." **CALVIN**

Calvin won the 400 meters and the 200 meters, but I was the high point man for the King City Invitational our senior year. I won the 100 meters and long jump and ran on the 4 x 100-meter and 4 x 400-meter relay teams. Calvin was the star, setting a record in the 400 meters, but I had more events that day. **ALVIN**

This certainly wasn't any fashion show. Alvin (left) and I put on our finest clothes for the North Salinas High School Track and Field Awards Ceremony following our sophomore season. I think we won just about everything that year. **CALVIN**

Just kicking back at the Bonnie Doone apartments in Salinas. That's Calvin with the No. 23 jersey. **ALVIN**

THIS WAS A 100-METER race during a high school invitational my sophomore year. Despite the bad form and skinny body, I won the race. The blond guy to my right in the Palma uniform is Matt Amaral, who also had an identical twin brother, Chad. **ALVIN**

WE WON THE STATE TITLE in the 4 x 400-meter relay with this group. That's me on the left with Bobby Porrez, Alvin and Jason Ball. This was at a time when Alvin and I were constantly trying to find a place to sleep and food to eat. The good thing was that some of our friends on the track team worked in fast food restaurants and they would hook us up with dinner. **CALVIN**

3

TRANSCONTINENTAL DRIFT

ALVIN

There were no tears during the ride back to the airport in San Jose. I looked out of the windows of my father's car. I saw the mountains, the fields of produce that helped make Salinas known as the country's salad bowl. The time there had been great. Calvin and I met friends, we slept in separate beds for the first time in our lives and for the first time we experienced a sense of stability. Meals were cooked, clothes were cleaned, support was given and was received. Still, there was a part of me that ached. I thought California was beautiful, but I became more and more homesick for my grandmother. After about three weeks, I had asked my father if I could go back home to Orlando. I knew more than anything that I wanted to live with my grandmother and take care of her. Nothing else really mattered at the time. I just couldn't wait to get back home and to be near her. I don't know whether it was so much that I didn't like California or that I just didn't like being in California with my grandmother in Florida by herself. So my father bought me a plane ticket and we all got into the car for the hour drive back along highway 101. I don't know how much I thought about the fact my brother would not be coming with me. We were kids, so I don't think I really understood the significance of the separation.

I remember that time as being different, but

not necessarily in a bad way. I guess we were forced to experience life on our own. We had to find other people to talk to, other friends with whom we could share feelings. Until that point, we always had one another. No matter what was going on we always could count on being together. We probably spent 95 percent of our time with each other from the time we were born until that year.

I just wasn't ready to settle in California. Calvin adjusted much more quickly. I was so homesick that nothing else mattered. Leaving Calvin behind was secondary. I knew it would be just the two of us, my grandmother and me in the house. I don't know where my mother was at the time, so I would do most of the cooking. I felt like we needed that time together emotionally and spiritually. My grandmother didn't understand why I didn't stay with my father. I never told her it was because I missed her too much.

CALVIN

I just remember the feeling being so different. I was so used to Alvin being with me at every school I ever had attended. Once he went back to Florida I felt uncomfortable. I wasn't scared, but I was lost. I didn't know anyone, and there is a big difference between the East Coast and the West Coast. For one thing, I never had gone to an integrated school. From the time I entered kindergarten in Florida until seventh grade we had attended all black schools. Here I am in eighth grade walking into a school in California with maybe 2 or 3 percent African-Americans. I had to find my way on every level and I was alone. Alvin was my friend and my companion. We walked to school together, ate lunch together, played together. I think I adjusted very well under the circumstances. I knew I couldn't depend on Alvin to walk me home from school or talk to me every day. I had four or five black friends that I hung out with initially. After a while I ventured out a little bit and a Mexican kid named Alfredo ended up being my best friend. I also had two little brothers, Albert, who was the older of the two, and Antonio. What really kept me going was sports. That's where I fit in. There was a program in physical education class with rewards. You had to accomplish certain goals to reach different levels. As you accomplished these goals you received different colored shorts. I never quite made it into the gold shorts, but I found out I had the ability to run fast. I started breaking some school records in different events. But track and field really wasn't something in the picture at that point. Music would have been a much more logical focus for me because my father was a musician on the side. I would play the keyboards and he bought me a drum machine to play with. It was around that time that I started writing songs. I wrote love songs primarily and a few rap songs. It wasn't like I was going to be a superstar or anything, but I liked the process. I still have three or four of the songs I wrote from that time.

ALVIN

My grandmother and I became each other's support system at that time. Spiritually, I grew so much that year. I started to feel my own independence because I was on my own to some extent. We were together, but I was the one doing the cooking, cleaning up the house, doing errands and helping her doing things. It opened me up to the possibility of becoming anything. Later on, I moved across town to Eatonville and lived with my father's mother, Josephine. I had a cousin over there and some friends, so going to school became fun again. I thought about Calvin all the time, but was realizing my independence.

CALVIN

Everything about Orlando looked different when I returned for the summer following eighth grade in Salinas. It was like I had been living in a colorized world and now I was returning to a place that was black and white. I went back to the house where we were raised in to see my grandmother and I couldn't wait to see Alvin. I enjoyed my year in California and I adjusted pretty easily. But I missed both of them more than I had imagined. Still, I couldn't stay in the old neighborhood. I didn't realize how bad our living conditions had been growing up until I lived with my father, who always kept everything clean and organized. I decided to live with my father's mother in Eatonville, which is one of the oldest black communities in America. I had a cousin over there and Alvin was staying there at the time, too. I knew I wanted to get back to California and be with my father, but as the summer ran into the start of school Alvin and I were still in Florida.

I was drawn to sports just like any other boy at that age, but it wasn't until we enrolled at Edgewater High School in Orlando for the start of our freshman year that I recognized my own competitiveness. Our grandmother told Alvin and me we should join the Junior R.O.T.C. She thought the discipline would be good for us and that the program would give us a foundation to build upon. Alvin and I quickly realized running fast was one of the ways you could distinguish yourself. I was small compared to the other kids. I was tall enough, but very thin. I felt like I had to find something that would set me apart. We were both at the age when we needed to find a way to stand out on our own. R.O.T.C. had Field Days which were physical fitness training days. We would run, do push-ups, sit-ups and a number of other activities designed to make us stronger and more fit. I quickly became the fastest runner in the group, which in turn earned me points toward a higher ranking. I remember feeling so much better about myself at that time. I had found something that set me apart and made me special. I walked taller, stuck out my chest a little more. For the first time in my life outside the presence of my grandmother, I felt special.

A L V I N

There was an 800-meter run and both of us were beating a senior who was supposed to be the best. The fact we could run fast made us recognized around the school. Now we had something no one else could take from us. We might not have had the right clothes or the right shoes, but we had something they couldn't acquire. Instead of focusing on the negatives, other kids looked at us differently.

School was going well but Calvin and I were talking about California all the time. I guess I figured that if we could stand out a little bit in Florida, who knows how good it might be to attend high school in California.

Calvin had told me all about his year in Salinas, the friends he made, the way he felt there. I was ready. The year apart had been good for both of us, but I wanted more. Late in the semester our dad called and asked if we wanted to come out for the Christmas break. Alvin and I had gone out for the football team, but we dropped out after getting the call from our dad. We had no intention of coming back to Florida. We might be going for Christmas, but that was only the beginning.

C A L V I N

Once we were with my dad, we knew our lives would be stable because that's just the way he was. Everything was clean, organized and put together. Those things were important to him and he knew we needed to be in an environment like that. Much of the order Alvin and I have in our own homes now comes from the time we spent with our father. He taught us the importance of the kinds of things most people take for granted: how to take care of ourselves, how to organize and manage our time, how to dress and conduct ourselves. No one had ever told us about these things before we lived with our dad. He kept our clothes nice and washed. And he cooked most of the meals. Our mom, she was doing other things most of the time. Our clothes weren't clean and neither were we sometimes. Our dad made sure that when we went to school we had a lunch box and lunch money. He knew the conditions we had lived in, and he wanted to expose us to something better.

Most importantly, we knew he cared. Even when he went to California when we were in sixth grade, he would call us. At Christmas he would send big boxes of gifts and other times just out of the blue we would receive a package in the mail. It might be a skateboard we wanted, or a card to let us know he was thinking about us. Although we would have preferred to have him be a larger part of our lives early on, we knew he was trying. He always made an effort to have a relationship with us. He wanted us to know he cared about our lives.

The only reason he wasn't around as much as he wanted when we were younger was because to some extent he was a victim of the circumstances of his own life. He had a role in some of those circumstances, but not all of them. He worked extremely hard to create something better for himself and for us. We actually lived with our father for a year or two during elementary school in Orlando. But our mother wanted to be in control of something and all she really could control at that time was us. She challenged him to assume the fatherly role, but once he did she realized that was not what she wanted at all. I think she had hoped he would fail, but he didn't. He might not have been there physically as much as we wanted, but we knew he loved us. That's a heck of a lot more than you can say for a lot of kids we grew up with. We knew our father loved us and we knew we were in his thoughts. Looking back, and now being a father myself, I know he was just trying to create an environment that fit the vision he had of himself. He had to be away to work and to get his life in order. But he always wanted us to be a part of what he was creating for himself. He knew how we

lived, the environment we were being raised in. He wanted something better for us and we knew that.

When Calvin and I returned to California it was like going to heaven. People liked us, we performed well in sports, girls talked to us. No one had any idea where we had come from, the shack we lived in, the dirty clothes, shoes two sizes too big, the neglect we felt from our own mother, all the craziness around the house and neighborhood. No one knew these things. It was a fresh start, a 180-degree turn for us. We went from being unfit in the eyes of our peers in Florida to fitting right in with everybody in Salinas. It was a whole new world, and it helped me understand why we're always told not to judge one another. I realized sometimes you have no idea what another person might have experienced. Our own experience taught us to open our minds and get to know people before we judge them. Looking back, if my dad had not gone to California, Florida and that life would have been the only life we would have known.

The east side of Salinas was considered the roughest part of town, but we lived on the right side of the tracks so to speak. There were serious gang problems at that time between the

Bloods and Crips. One of the first days of school at North Salinas High, Calvin was wearing a red checkered Pendleton jacket like lumberjacks wore. It turned out that was what the gangsters wore in Salinas. Calvin and I just wore them because they were in style. So these gangsters came up to Calvin and me and started asking us questions. "Are you down with red? Or are you down with blue? What do you claim?" We didn't realize it at the time, but the Crips wore blue and the Bloods wore red. Calvin and I looked at each other and we really didn't know what all that stuff was about. I said, "I claim Florida. That's where we're from." They knew by that comment we had no damn clue as to what they were talking about. We were fortunate enough to stay away from all the gang activity because we had a lot of positive support at the time. We were living with my father and he told us to stay away from that stuff, and we had teachers and coaches talking to us all the time about the gangs. Salinas had one of the worst gang problems in the country in the early 1990s. At one point Salinas had one of the highest murder rates in the nation. These guys were killing each other left and right. There was a low income apartment complex not far from our complex that was the Northern California version of a ghetto. It didn't look anything like the neighborhood we came from but it was in an extremely dangerous part of town. That's where all the gangsters lived and hung out. The fact we played sports from the time we enrolled in high school really eliminated any opportunity of becoming involved in the gangs. It was like gang bangers had an understanding or respect for guys playing on the sports teams. They knew you were trying to accomplish something. We played basketball, football and track so our time was pretty much spoken for. Most gangsters had girlfriends who were in gangs too, so after school they would just hang out. But they were rough. For new members they had this ritual called Jumping You In. If you wanted to be in one of the gangs you had to take a whipping from all the other guys in the gang. I'm talking about taking punches to the face by a bunch of guys who are about to become your new friends. It was crazy. You would see guys coming to school with blacks eyes, busted lips. That stuff would go on right at school sometimes. Ironically, I understood the lure of the gangs by playing sports. We had a place to be praised, to be a part of something. Those guys had to find support and positive reinforcement from one another, and they usually earned that respect by doing something violent to push themselves to the front of the pack. We could do the same thing but we were doing it on a playing field. The tough guy of the group just wanted to be recognized as being somebody. That's not much different from trying to excel on the track or football field. For all the gang activity, North Salinas High School was still a long way from the Orlando ghetto we had called home.

C A L V I N

We went home to visit our grandmother after finishing our freshman year, but we didn't stay long. By then I considered myself a Californian. I loved everything about Salinas, the natural beauty, the way we were treated, the living conditions and support. I think Alvin and I were looking forward to our sophomore year in high school more than any other year in our lives. We went out for the football team but really didn't play that much, although I felt like I should have played a lot. We played basketball too. When spring came we went out for the track team.

No one knew what to expect, including our-

selves when the track season rolled around. We had been fast running against guys in R.O.T.C. in Florida, but we had no idea how much talent we actually had for track and field. I gravitated to the 200 meters and 400 meters right away. Alvin focused on the 100 meters and the long jump. Neither of us really knew what we were doing because we never had had any serious instruction. We just ran when it was time to run.

Even though we started winning almost all the time, I still didn't understand how good we were. I was running in the low 46 seconds for 400 meters, which was extremely fast for that age group. There weren't many college runners doing 46 seconds in the 400 meters on a regular basis, and here I was running the race for the first time and pushing 46 seconds. Alvin was having just as much success in the 100 meters and long jump. He was running 10.6 to 10.8 in the 100 and long jumping 21 or 22 feet on pure natural ability. We were going so fast so consistently that we became well known all over Northern California.

It was like every time Calvin ran he was breaking a record. Every dual meet, every invitational, Calvin established a new record. I don't think there was a single meet that year that Calvin didn't break the record in the 400 meters. I set a couple records in the 100 meters, but Calvin was winning everything. It was a wonderful time because we were doing the kinds of things well-adjusted kids did all over the country. We were going to school, we had friends, we were excelling in sports and we had support at home. In fact, everyone knew who our dad was because he always would be in the stands with a video camera. He was extremely proud of what we were doing in school and on the track. Once in a while he would have all the guys over to the apartment for hot dogs and things like that. It seemed like everything was coming together for us.

We thought our sophomore year was really just a taste of what we could accomplish. The coaches thought so too. For two guys who never had competed in organized sports before, we dominated. And neither one of us really knew what we were doing. We didn't have a formal training program in the off-season and our techniques were still a long way from being sophisticated. I don't think we really understood what that kind of success could mean to us down the road. College still seemed like a long way off and the idea of being recruited to run for a major university wasn't a part of our thought process. We knew we had done well, but I really don't think we had any idea of just how fast we were running at that age.

We stayed through the summer and our lives had more order than they ever had had. We were looking forward to our junior year because Alvin and I were going to go out for the football team, and we knew we could become starters. School was going well too, and we had a lot of friends. But early in that school year my father received a call from Florida. His mother, Josephine, had diabetes and no one knew how much longer she might live. I guess we were used to the disruptions in our lives, but I don't think either of us could have predicted how deeply the next move would affect us.

When the Christmas break came we all packed up and moved back to Florida. Our father wanted to be sure his mother didn't pass away while he was on the other side of the country. He wanted to be there to take care of her if something should happen. That says something about the kind of person he is. I don't know how many people would pack up and drive across the country just to be able to help their mother through her final days. But that's what happened. So just as we were finding our stride so to speak, we were back in a car traveling across the country to Florida.

Once we got to Florida all Alvin and I thought about was getting back to California. The Christmas break ended and we didn't even enroll in school in Florida. We had no intention of staying there and we were trying to make that point. I had a friend in California named Michael Jones and we stayed in touch during that time. One day I called Magic, which is what we called him, and asked if he thought his mother would let us stay with them. She didn't say no, but she wasn't too thrilled with the idea

either. Eventually she kind of agreed, which was the opening we needed. We talked to our dad and pretty soon we were getting on a bus for Northern California. He didn't think it was a good idea, but he supported our decision because he knew what California meant to us.

ALVIN

We were 16 years old and we had all our belongings in two bags. At that time, the bus took four days to get to Salinas from Orlando. There were no showers, and the bathrooms were disgusting because of all the people using them. But we had enough money for snacks along the way and it was very scenic. Besides, we were going back to the one place where we were somebody. People knew us in Salinas and we had friends, boys and girls. We really weren't sure how we would survive, but we knew we would find our way.

We didn't go to school right away when we got back to Salinas. There was this sense of complete freedom. We were teenagers completely on our own. We eventually enrolled at North Salinas High School for what was left of our junior year. But the adventure was slowly becoming more difficult. Our housing situation deteriorated to the point where we spent most days just trying to survive. We moved 11 times between our arrival in Salinas and the start of track season our senior year. In between we slept in cars, on floors and just about any place with a roof.

One of the places we lived was back at the Bonnie Doone apartment complex. We had met Tenisha when we lived there with our father. She was much older, about 28. But we would talk to her all the time and we became good friends. She had a little girl and she was real cool, like a good older sister. So we would hang out at her apartment sometimes, watching television or just talking. Tenisha started dating Chris, who had just been released from the army. She introduced us as her little brothers, and we all got along really well. Chris was 28 or 29 at the time. He was in the middle of a divorce, and he was trying to decide whether he wanted to move back to Georgia where he was from. Every morning about the same time, he would come by Tenisha's apartment and we would just roll around with him all day listening to music. Tenisha wound up moving back to Bakersfield, so we moved in with Chris until he left for Georgia. He still had a couple months left on his apartment lease, so he let us stay there until it ran out. When it came time to move out of Chris's apartment, we moved in with Cory and his mother. We were almost done with our junior year in high school during all this. And we were not exactly great students because we were more focused on surviving day to day than trying to get passing grades in school. We also didn't have any support. Our father was 3,000 miles away and we didn't have any family anywhere near us. So we were moving constantly from one house to another. We even lived in a car for a while that had the back window broken out. We had to put plastic over the window, and you wouldn't believe what that sounded like when it was raining. There were four of us living in that car for about two weeks because we would only find a house to stay in for a day or two at a time.

It was all real. We were on our own just trying to put one foot in front of the other every day. I think the thing that kept us going was each other. Also, we were really into music at the time. Music became the glue to some degree because school wasn't a high priority given our lives. Looking back, it was like a high schooler's dream. We woke up whenever we wanted, went to school some of the time. I mean, no one was watching. We were completely on our own. We had so many issues in our lives at the time that going to school was another one at the end of a long list. Still, we almost had it together at the beginning of our senior year. We met Jeff, an older guy who was into music, and we lived with him for a while. At the time, we were hanging around with musicians all the time and music represented our only hope. We were all looking to be rappers or R&B singers and songwriters. We knew it was a dream, but it was all we had to hang on to. We all had different equipment and we believed music represented our best chance to find our place. The music is really what kept us sane.

We didn't have any idea what was going on back in Florida because we didn't have a phone and every day was consumed with trying to survive. We were trying to get something together and there wasn't anyone back there who could do anything for us. We knew the financial situation of our father and the rest of the family, and we didn't have anything positive to report anyway. So there we were alone and bouncing around trying to find a warm blanket and a bowl of hot soup. Besides, we were embarrassed by the entire situation, and we didn't have the heart to tell our grandmother because we knew she would tell us to come on back home. We just couldn't do that at the time. I think we had a sense that everything would be all right eventually. We just didn't know when. As it turned out it took a lot longer than either of us could have imagined. That hope is really all we had to keep us going.

CALVIN

I played football my senior year and we were on the track team the following January. We looked at sports as just an activity, something we liked to do. We really couldn't see sports for anything more than what they were at the time because we were busy trying to survive all the time. Alvin and I joined the track team because we wanted to be part of something. We had run track as sophomores and we did pretty well, so we knew we could contribute. The whole team just came together in part because we inspired everybody. I wanted attention. I wanted to be known for something positive, and that's where I found my place and self worth at the time. I never realized how fast I was going, and I didn't really have any context for what we were doing on the track. I knew Alvin and I were winning everything and the team was great, but I didn't understand the fact I was running faster than any high school kid had ever run before anywhere in the world. I knew we were in the newspapers a lot, but the best thing about starting to stand out in the city was that more people knew us. We had friends working at fast-food places who would give us food on the side and things like that because they knew us from the newspapers.

ALVIN

Calvin was running times as a high school senior that guys were running on the international circuit in 2000. That's how fast he was. And neither of us knew what we were doing. You have to remember, our primary focus still was trying to survive, to find a place to sleep and to find some warm food. There was nobody around who could help us understand what the opportunity might be after high school. It wasn't that we didn't take our accomplishments seriously, we just had more pressing needs. We did help our team to the state championship. It was the first time any school from our area had won the state title. Calvin ran the show. He won the 200 and the 400 and helped win two relays.

CALVIN

Even with all that success in track our personal lives away from school were the same. We didn't have any direction or guidance, and we were constantly moving around. So once the track season ended we really just stopped going to school. Our highlight, our graduation, was the state track and field meet. We fell far behind on the number of credits we needed to graduate because of what had happened our junior year. It wasn't like we could attend summer school to catch up because of our living conditions, or lack of living conditions. Still, there were all kinds of schools contacting our high school about Alvin and me going to college. All the big schools, USC, UCLA, Oregon and even Ivy League colleges like Columbia, wanted us to play football and run track. But we didn't have the grades or anything else going for us to make that kind of move. And we didn't even have a clue about what it might mean for us.

But we kept having success on the track, this time on a national basis. I won the 400 meters at the United States Junior Nationals, and Alvin and I ran a leg on the gold-medal-winning 4 x 400-meter relay.

ALVIN

Coach Shaw was the head track coach at Hartnell Community College in Salinas. He had watched us our entire senior year and he wanted us to run track at Hartnell. Calvin and I didn't have anything else going for us at the time, so Coach Shaw helped arrange financial aid. It turned out to be a blessing because the money allowed us to get an apartment at the Mariner Village Apartments. We had two roommates, and the four of us shared all the bills.

I remember feeling like everything was starting to work out. We had our own apartment, we each cooked and cleaned. It was like we were a family. We gave out candy to kids on Halloween. It was the first time we had our own home. We had our own keys. We could come home when we wanted, leave when we wanted. We had cable, so we could watch television instead of watching cars all day. We had phones so we could get phone calls. It was like we had graduated to freedom. We were back in school, running for the track team. Life was definitely looking up.

I QUALIFIED for the semifinals in this race at the 1996 Olympic Trials in Atlanta. I remember feeling pretty good at this point. I was confident I could make the team, but the pressure started to build after this quarterfinal race. **ALVIN**

I felt great the first two days of the 1996 Trials. I qualified for the semifinals, but I got a little over anxious on the third day. I started running another guy's race in the semifinals and I missed qualifying for the finals by 7/1000ths of a second. **CALVIN**

THE PRESSURE

STARTED TO BUILD

THE BRUCE JENNER CLASSIC was the first 400-meter race I ever ran against international competition. It was about three months before the 1996 Olympic Trials and no one thought I had a chance against that field because there were a number of past Olympians in the race . . . I'm running right along with everyone else at the first turn. I'm thinking, "OK, I can run with these guys." We're now on the backstretch at 200 meters and I can hear one of my friends call my name. I'm even seeing some of my friends in the stands. That's how inexperienced I was. I really wasn't even concentrating completely. At the top of the turn, 300 meters, I'm in fifth position and we're coming off the turn toward the homestretch. I realize that I'm still energized. So I pushed and I started to pass one guy after another. At 40 meters I catch Darnell Hall, who was a big name internationally in the 400 meters. No one was really close to Michael Johnson at that point but Darnell was the closest. I went right past Darnell and held on coming through the finish line. The crowd is going crazy, my coach is going nuts, my brother is screaming and yelling. It felt good to be a winner. I went 45.12, my personal record to that point. **ALVIN**

I GOT CRITICIZED by all kinds of people who didn't think I had a chance because of my lack of experience in the 400 meters. All that turned out to be a source of fire for me. I trained night and day. I ran in the rain, the cold weather. I would wake up in the middle of the night, slip on my shoes and jog around the city. I was so focused on the 1996 Olympics and there were so many people that didn't think I had a chance, that I was driven. I admit that given what had happened to Calvin and me in 1994 and 1995, trying to make the 1996 United States Olympic Team probably seemed far fetched. But both of us had that sense of pursuit instilled in us by our grandmother. That's what I called on in those training sessions. She always said, "Alvin, no matter what you do, be the best. Even if you're going to be a liar, be the best." What more can you ask for? I would think about that at practice, the negative things people said to me along the way. Even my coach, Gary Shaw, didn't think I had a chance. **ALVIN**

I WAS SCARED from the first round to the last in the 1996 Olympic Trials at Atlanta. As I advanced through the rounds I didn't even know how to act. It was a humbling experience. I didn't have any idea of what to expect, but I knew I could run with those guys. Michael Johnson (left) finished first in the Olympic Trials 400-meter finals, I finished third and Butch Johnson (right) finished second. I was right behind two guys who had set the world record for the 400 meters. **ALVIN**

I WAS SO EXCITED

I JUST RECEIVED the baton from LaMont Smith in the 4 x 400-meter relay finals at the 1996 Olympics in Atlanta. You re still running 400 meters but in a relay you are just trying to blow it out. **ALVIN**

THAT I JUST SCREAMED WHEN I TOOK OFF

I RAN THE SECOND LEG of the gold-medal-winning 4 x 400-meter relay in the 1996 Olympics in Atlanta and gave us a four-meter lead. I'm handing the stick (baton) to Derek Mills. Anthuan Maybank ran the final leg. The 4 x 400-meter relay isn't nearly as technically challenging as the 4 x 100-meter relay. In our race, I'm judging everything by sight. I'm watching the guy in front of me and I'm adjusting to him. In the 4 x 100-meter relay everything is going full speed. Those guys are doing 9.8 second splits and handing off to a guy who's sprinting at near top speed. **ALVIN**

FOLLOWING OUR VICTORY in the 4 x 400-meter relay in 1996, five of us took a victory lap with American flags. LaMont Smith is on the left, I'm holding my daughter, Shiyah, who was two at the time, Derek Mills and Anthuan Maybank are the other two runners in uniform. The guy in back is Jason Rouseau, who beat out Calvin by 7/1000ths of a second in the semifinals of the Olympic Trials. **ALVIN**

WHAT I REMEMBER MOST about being on the stand and receiving the gold medal in 1996 was a sense of joy and relief. All the pressure was off. We had run the race without incident. I felt fulfilled. From left to right, our winning team of Anthuan Maybank, me, Lamong Smith (looking up) and Derek Mills bows to the crowd. **ALVIN**

A SENSE OF JOY AND RELIEF

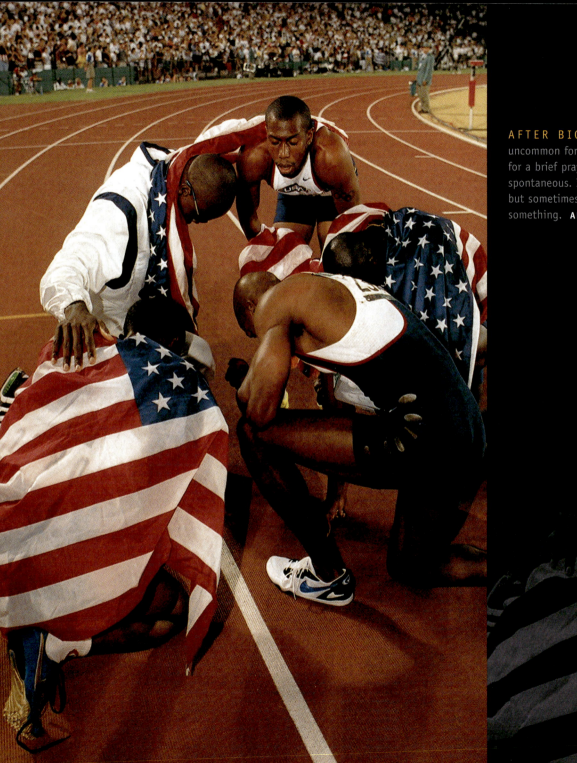

4

HOME ALONE

A L V I N

The cushions of the couch fit in between a pine frame. The carpet below my feet was nice, clean. The walls were an off-white and the television, a small color set, remained off. It was late afternoon but it felt like three in the morning. As I sat there in the quiet of another apartment we called home, I could feel the past rolling into that room like a wave. Calvin and I had been forced out of the apartment at Mariner Village when our two friends left. The bills became too much to handle and we could feel the walls moving in on us again. We had landed in this place with two other friends, both of whom would be leaving in the coming weeks. Though we were still going to school at Hartnell, we were slowly falling back into the search-and-survive mode. Our financial aid had run out and we knew it was just a matter of time before our situation deteriorated further. My Nissan Sentra, which had started the day in the parking lot outside, had been repossessed just an hour before. A week earlier I had decided to use what money I had to get the car fixed. That money would have made the car payment. I was 20 years old but I felt like an old man sitting on that couch. I was exhausted and the thought of going back out on the streets to chase down another place to live was too much. As the questions rolled around in my head so did an answer. Why was this happening? What lessons were we supposed to have learned? Did we learn them? Why couldn't we live in a nice two-story house with a car in the driveway? I wanted to go home, and the only home I knew was back in Orlando.

C A L V I N

When Alvin went back to Florida I felt lost. I knew how difficult staying would be, but I also knew everything Orlando represented in our lives. I knew I could live with Alvin at my father's house, but I wanted to hold on by myself. For a while I did. I worked at the rodeo with a guy who had a lemonade concession. We would go to fairs, arts and crafts shows and things like that to sell lemonade. I didn't know what to do at that time so I tried to do anything to keep busy. I also worked for a moving and storage company that eventually led me back to Florida.

I was a passenger in a little Ford Ranger when the truck was hit head-on by a Ford F-150. The F-150 came straight into our lane and hit us square. I was sitting in the center, one of my former high school football coaches was driving and a guy named Armando was in the passenger seat to my right. We had pallets in the back of the truck and they crashed through the back window. The impact knocked the driver unconscious. I didn't know if he was dead or alive. I moved my knees, which had slammed into the dashboard. I could feel the glass in my back and the back of my neck. Armando's injuries were limited to the glass that punctured his skin. I ended up with serious whiplash.

I took the money from the insurance settlement and bought a black 1989 four-cylinder, two-door Mustang. It wasn't new, but it was the first car either one of us had owned free and clear. I didn't need another sign. It was time to head back across the country. I jumped into that car with $200 and drove from Northern California to Orlando straight through in three days. I spent about $130 on gas and still had around $70 when I got back home.

A L V I N

I found a job near Orlando working on an assembly line putting together vending machines. I was living with my father and I used his car to commute about 30 minutes each morning and up to 90 minutes each night. I arrived in the morning, grabbed my time card and punched in along with everyone else. I slipped on a protective apron and lifted the safety glasses to cover my eyes. Then I took my place for the next eight hours and worked on vending machines. I was working with older people primarily but there were some younger guys trying to make a living. The older guys had done this kind of work their whole lives. The younger guys were hoping to do the same thing. I remember looking around at their faces one afternoon on payday. Everyone was so excited to be getting paid. They were truly happy. I didn't have anything at the time so I understood their joy. But I remember saying to myself, "Man, this is not for me. There has to be more." These people worked hard and they were doing the best they could to create a life for themselves and their families. There was nothing wrong with that. It just wasn't how I saw my life unfolding.

Although I was still trying to produce and write music, I was slowly getting tired all over again from the monotony. My grandmother had always told us to "be somebody." That didn't mean the men and women I worked with shouldn't have been proud of the work they did. For the most part, my coworkers were good people. My family didn't have a great history to say the least. But I knew I didn't belong there. About the only thing I knew for sure at the time was that if there was going to be any hope or future for our family, then Calvin and I were the ones that had to make it happen. My story was not going to end on an assembly line in Orlando.

C A L V I N

When I got back to the Carve Shores District in Orlando and walked into that house on Lennox Boulevard and Aaron Avenue, everything looked different. We had a good name around the neighborhood because of what we had done on the track in California. The guys we grew up with looked at us and saw something we didn't see. Compared to most of them, we had a talent for doing something other than selling drugs or hustling on the street corners. These guys looked up to Alvin and me at a time when we were looking up at the rest of the world. I got a job at a department store working in the sporting goods section and moved in with Alvin at my dad's house. The house was extremely crowded, but I didn't have much choice. Besides, I didn't have to spend my days looking for a roof and a blanket.

A L V I N

Before long our lives seemed to be running into our past. The temptation to chase the easy money being made by drug dealers in our neighborhood became more real with every passing day. Our childhood friends were selling dope and we all knew there was fast money to be made. We slowly started slipping into the mindset that it was either going to be the assembly line or selling dope. Those guys were making three times what we were making doing our jobs. We could feel the temptation, the lure of that life. The road to that point had been so hard and the money to be made looked easy. We knew the gangs because we lived around them growing up. We knew we could get in and make some quick money. We also knew the risks. Guys were going to jail, prison, getting shot, being killed. But we saw guys we knew rolling around in new cars with nice clothes, nice watches, beautiful girls sitting next to them, and here we were working 40 hours a week for a paycheck every two weeks. The temptation became so real and it was right there in front of us. Before it could get a grasp and a firm hold, we decided we had to leave. If we stayed in Orlando, we knew what we would become.

CALVIN

Deep down, California always seemed to represent a positive alternative. In retrospect, it seems like God brought us down to Florida to show us what real struggle looked like. It's like He wanted us to sit back and observe that life. When we were moving from place to place in Salinas, we thought we understood the low side of life. Then we went back to Florida and saw the true picture of hopelessness. We had it hard trying to make our way alone in California, but we didn't have it that hard.

ALVIN

I'm on an assembly line. Calvin is selling sporting goods. Dope selling is all around. Guys are shooting and killing one another everywhere. Cops are beating up guys. Other guys are trying to shoot cops. Girls are setting up their own boyfriends to get robbed. This is what we had all around us all the time. And it wasn't like we were reading about these things in newspapers. We knew these people. We watched it happen. Still, we were slowly getting sucked in. We were adapting to our surroundings to some degree and we had even bought a gun. It's not hard to see how it could have happened to Calvin and me. Our boys, the guys we had grown up with, were all selling dope. We knew they weren't going anywhere good with their lives, but we saw the things they had that we had never even been close to having. It took a head-on collision just for one of us to get a car we could call our own. There are guns all over the place and we're getting introduced to this life through our friends. We're still working at our jobs and we know the reality of that life, but the temptation only became stronger. Ultimately, one event put everything back into perspective. I was sitting in a car with my girlfriend and playing with the gun. She was in the driver's seat turned toward me with her back resting against the door. I had a small .38, a six shooter. I had emptied the chambers. I knew I had counted six bullets right there on the seat. I'm sitting on the passenger side, leaning against the door and we're talking. I have the gun in my hand and I'm just playing with it, pulling the trigger because I know it's empty. So we're just talking and, click, I pull the tigger. We keep talking and, click, I pull the trigger again. Then, Pow!, the gun goes off and blows a hole right in the floorboard a fraction of an inch from my right foot. At that instant I said, "I have to get out of here. I have to get Calvin, get in that Mustang and get to California." She was scared. I was scared. I went upstairs to this apartment complex where my little sister, Africia, lived and I sold that gun to the first person I saw. I didn't care how much money I got. I just wanted to get rid of the gun. To me that entire incident was a blessing. It was almost like we were birds in a cage in Florida and all we wanted to do was get out because we knew we would die in that cage if we didn't.

CALVIN

There was too much of the past and no future for us in Orlando. As hard as I thought it was in California, that's where I felt most free. There was a sense of being able to become whatever you wanted to be there versus feeling trapped by your own history in Florida. The more we thought about California, the more we realized our real family had been there. We had friends, teachers and coaches, people who genuinely cared about us and what we were doing. In Florida, everybody was down for themselves. No one cared about one another. Our father and our grandmother cared about us, but there was only so much they could do. The larger support structure in Florida didn't exist the way it did in California.

ALVIN

The difference was that in California we had people trying to make a connection to help us understand our potential. Coach Shaw would explain his life experiences to help us better understand what we had to do to improve our lives. The dope dealers wouldn't share the dark side of their lives. They wouldn't tell you anything about getting shot, or being arrested, or facing prison time. None of those guys told me anything about what could happen. And they didn't care who they took down with them. You could be riding in a car with a guy who had a kilo of cocaine under the seat and he wouldn't say a word. We realized there were people trying to look out for us in California. They were telling us the things we needed to know.

CALVIN

I talked to Alvin about track and field and the possibility of using our talents to create an opportunity for ourselves. The fact that we hadn't run competitively much less trained for more than a year didn't seem like a big deal given what our lives were at the time. I told Alvin the Olympics were coming up in 1996 and if we could make the United States Olympic Team things might turn around. This was early 1995 and the Olympics didn't seem any more ridiculous than driving across the country without a job or a place to live. I had run qualifying times in the 400 meters in high school. I knew that if we trained hard, we'd have a chance to make the U.S. Team.

ALVIN

I think Calvin felt more confident with his track skills than I did. We didn't have any idea that what we were talking about was a one in a million chance. We were in a place mentally and emotionally where we couldn't stop and dwell on the negatives. Why shouldn't we think we could make the Olympic Team? We had gone through so much in a little over two years that training for the Olympics didn't seem that crazy to us. Of course, the day-to-day issues of staying alive once again took most of our mental, emotional and spiritual energy.

CALVIN

When we got back to Salinas I looked up a girl I had dated in high school, Marie. I knew she was the kind of friend I could count on. Her father, Robert Domingos, was a teacher and a professional pianist. Marie asked him if I could stay with them for a few days while Alvin and I figured out our lives. He agreed and I found out why Marie was the way she was. Her father treated me as one of the family while I was there. Neither one of us knew what was ahead, but that brief stop at Mr. Domingos's house made the coming transition that much smoother.

Alvin found a place to stay for a few nights with a friend, too. But within a week we knew we were on our own. There was a hill a few miles up the road from Marie's house. We decided to park the car there. The first night we parked facing down that hill. We sat inside across the street from a small ranch house that had cows behind it in a field. To our right was a dried up creek bed lined with pine trees and weeds. We chose that spot because hardly anyone drove through that area. We had some blankets and we flipped a coin. Alvin would get the backseat. I would sleep in the front. No big deal, we thought. One or two nights in the car was nothing we hadn't done before. We just knew everything would become clear in a day or so, three or four days at the most. We could handle a couple days in the car. No problem. At first, it was even kind of fun.

ALVIN

The first night was easy. By the third night it had started to become old. By the end of the first week we didn't know if the situation would ever improve. That's when reality started to set in. Pretty soon three weeks had gone by and we were still sleeping in that Mustang every night. Every morning I looked up at the sky and asked God, "How much longer?" It seemed like no matter what we tried to do to get out of that car, it wouldn't happen. Calvin tried to get a job, I tried to get a job. Nothing came easy because we didn't have a phone, much less an address. I started to wonder whether our family was cursed. I asked myself all kinds of questions. Are we paying for something our ancestors did? Is this the way it's going to be for Calvin and me? I had visions of people on the street pulling cardboard boxes over their heads. Are we going to be pushing a shopping cart and holding out a cup when we're 50 years old? I knew how those things could happen because I had seen them happen in our family. As the weeks passed and the first month turned into the second, I knew we could slip all the way down to rock bottom.

CALVIN

I remember the feeling of the sun coming up. We had blankets, but we couldn't keep the heat on all night. I can still feel the sun warming my face like it did every morning on that hill. I would stretch out by flexing my thigh and back muscles. Alvin would unwind his body in the backseat, his legs straightening between the two seats. Usually we wouldn't say a word for a few minutes. As bad as it was in that car, at least we had one another for support and comfort. We also had friends. I would get up in the morning and go down to Marie's house when her father left for work. I'd shower and have some breakfast. Sometimes I'd wash my clothes there. Alvin was seeing Marie's friend Stacy and he would go to her house and do the same. We were embarrassed by the situation but we tried to conduct ourselves as normally as possible under the circumstances. But the longer I slept in the car, the more my mind started to question everything. Just like Alvin, I had to confront the possibility that this would be my life.

ALVIN

We were living in a fantasy world inside that car. We even took what little money we had and bought lottery tickets. We had to face reality if we were going to get anywhere and that's what reading the Bible helped us to do. Calvin and I read the entire Bible sitting in that car. I had a little green one and Calvin's was red. They were small pocket-sized versions but we read every page at least once. Most of the time we would talk with one another through the night fantasizing about big houses, our dream cars and the possibility of becoming famous musicians or entertainers. We were selling each other on these dreams. All the while we were waiting for somebody to drop by the car with enough money to change our lives.

C A L V I N

I was praying someone would come along and literally take me out of the situation. I prayed and prayed but I was looking for a miracle. I finally realized that the answer was right in front of me. This mysterious secret to life we are all trying to find starts with the individual. You can gain insight from prayer and studying the Bible, but it was up to me and Alvin to do something with that information. Looking through the newspaper one day, I found an ad for a painting job. By now we had been in the car almost three weeks. We had spent our days looking for jobs, hanging out with our girlfriends and hiking through the hills and mountains. It wasn't until I started painting that everything became clear. I realized I was able bodied. I had arms, legs, feet. I was strong. I was young. It's

like I finally understood the answer to all our problems and it all boiled down to us. We had to create our destiny. No one was going to hand it to us. We had to go out and use everything we had been given to make our life happen. Otherwise, we were going to end up on the street or in that car.

As the spring moved into early summer, I started to feel energized again. Although Alvin and I were still living in the car, we were working as personal trainers at a 24-hour fitness club. Most of the time that's where we took our showers. One day in May I was working out at a local gym when I was called to the phone. Marie had been in an accident. A few months earlier we had found out she was pregnant and expecting to give birth in September. I ran out of the gym and jumped into the Mustang. The accident had taken place on Hillcrest Road. As I approached the scene I was shocked to see the car. It had been destroyed beyond repair. I knew our lives were about to become even more connected through the birth of our son, Jarijah. At that moment the thought of losing her was terrifying. I jumped out of my car and ran into the crowd. As I tried to make sense of the chaos, I saw some paramedics going into a nearby house. I ran up to the home and saw Marie inside. I looked into her eyes and seemed to know there was nothing seriously wrong. She spent the night in the hospital, but the baby was fine and so was Marie. That accident, like the one that produced the Mustang Alvin and I called home, helped change our lives. The insurance company gave Marie a few thousand dollars and we used the money to get an apartment. Pretty soon I found a better job selling shoes at the Big 5 Sporting Goods store. When Marie and I were settled, I contacted my old high school track coach, Ed Barber.

A L V I N

There was a story I remember reading in the Bible that helped me understand what we were supposed to do. The Lord gives three guys a number of talents. To the first man he gives five talents. The second man gets three talents, and the third man gets one talent. They are sent out into the world to see what they can do with these talents. When they return the Lord asks the first man what he has done with his talents. The man responds that he used his talents to improve and increase what he had been given. The Lord is pleased with this response and gives the man five more talents. The second man says the same thing and the Lord gives him three additional talents. Then the Lord asks the last man what he has done with his one talent. The man says, "The talent you gave me was so precious and I loved it so much that I dug a hole and I put my talent in the hole so no one could see it and therefore try to

take it away from me." The Lord tells the man he's a fool and takes away his only talent. I realized we were just like the last guy. We had talent, but we had been fools.

Given what we had been through and our lack of training, we were probably in the one place on earth capable of nurturing our dreams. There were coaches in Salinas who had seen us from the beginning and they understood our potential even better than we did. I can't imagine finding the kind of help anywhere else that we had available to us in Northern California.

Calvin and I decided to find separate coaches so we wouldn't be competing with one another. I went to see Gary Shaw, who had been our track coach at Hartnell Community College. Coach Shaw knew what I was capable of doing, but even he didn't think I had a chance of qualifying for the Olympic Team in the 400 meters. I had been a sprinter running the 100 meters and 200 meters in high school and college. But I chose the 400 meters because that was the race Calvin ran. I had confidence in myself because of what Calvin had been able to do in that race. Coach Shaw listened to me talk and then said, "Alvin, if you are serious, I want to coach you." I didn't tell him anything about what I had been through in the past year. I really just tried to make him feel like my life had been fine.

I contacted Coach Barber and we agreed to meet at his house for lunch. He had a nice place with a pool table. His two children were running around the house. I remember thinking how nice and orderly everything was there. I told him what Alvin and I wanted to do and the fact that Alvin was going to train with Coach Shaw. Coach Barber was excited because he had coached me in high school and he believed I was capable of making the Olympic Team. I don't know what the response would have been had I gone to a coach who had never seen me run. Right away Coach Barber started creating a program for me. I was in better shape than might be expected of someone who had spent more than two months living in a car. Alvin and I had spent many days running and hiking in the mountains. Not only did we feel comfortable with nature, but it was an activity that didn't require money.

Coach Shaw told me the top 20 400-meter runners in 1995 all ran faster than 46 seconds with at least 15 of them running 45 seconds or better. At the time I had never run faster than 46.23 for 400 meters. As a result, Coach Shaw told me to look at the 400-meter hurdles because of my athletic ability and speed. He figured that if it took me another two seconds to go over the hurdles, then I could probably run a little over 48 seconds, which would have put me in the game. I had never run hurdles before at any level, but I caught on quickly. Before long I was able to use the same step sequence Edwin Moses, the greatest 400-meter hurdler of all time, had used. Coach Shaw was amazed at how fast I was learning. I just wanted to make the Olympic Team.

But the hurdles were demanding for someone who had never run them before. I developed a deep groin injury because that race was so different from the kind of running I had done to that point. The injury turned out to be a blessing in disguise. I told Coach Shaw I needed to concentrate on the 400 meters because my body wasn't adjusting to the strain of the hurdles. We were about a third of the way through the season when I made the change and I was criticized by all kinds of people. No one, including Coach Shaw, thought I had a chance in the 400 meters because of my lack of experience. The negativity turned out to be a source of fire for me. I trained night and day. I ran in the rain, cold weather, early in the morning and late at night. I would wake up in the middle of the night, slip on my shoes and jog around the city. I was so focused on the Olympics, and there were so many people who didn't think I had a chance, that I was driven. I admit that given what had happened to Calvin and me in the year leading up to 1996 the Olympics seemed far-fetched. But both of us had a sense of pursuit instilled in us by our grandmother. That's what I called on in those training sessions. She always said, "Alvin, no matter what you do, be the best. Even if you're going to be a liar, be the best." That's what I carried with me.

CALVIN

I went to work every day at the sporting goods store and stood on my feet for eight hours selling shoes. When five o'clock came I'd head to the track to meet Coach Barber and train. I was surviving and doing what I thought it took to make the United States Olympic Team. It was like my life was gathering momentum. My son was born in September, Marie and I were able to pay the bills and a family was forming. On the track I could feel myself getting stronger.

The first break came when Coach Shaw and Coach Barber talked to one of the organizers of the Reno Air Games, an indoor meet in early 1996. The meet was on regional television and I was able to get an invitation to compete in the 400 meters. Reno wasn't far from Northern California and there were people who still remembered what I had done in high school. I knew I was ready to test my skills. I'm not sure what anyone else expected, but I went to Reno expecting to win. And that's exactly what I did. I ended up meeting and signing with an agent, who got me a small deal with Nike. The extra money was nice, but now I was on the road to the Olympic Trials. A few months later at the Nike Prefontaine Classic at the University of Oregon, I passed Roger Black, one of the best 400-meter runners in the world, down the stretch to win that event in a personal record of 44.74. That time qualified me for the Olympic Trials in Atlanta. The dream no longer seemed far-fetched or out of the question. It was slowly coming into view.

ALVIN

I found a job at a chemical company in Salinas and trained at night with Coach Shaw on the Hartnell track. The company made a chemical called "Etch," which is a compound that eats the copper off computer boards so the copper can be recycled. I was doing a little of everything. I mixed the chemicals for a while, worked in recycling, kept inventory, stocked inventory with a forklift. I had a nice apartment, decent clothes and a much clearer view of my future. For the first time in a long time, I felt like I had a sense of stability in my life. I could hold on to that job and chase my dream. Given where Calvin and I had been a few months earlier, that was all I needed to keep moving forward.

For me, the break came in San Jose at the Bruce Jenner Classic. Since I was a local guy, my coach was able to get me invited to run the 400 meters. To that point I had never run a 400-meter race against international competition. The field had a number of past Olympians and no one thought I had a chance. I saw it differently. The race was in our backyard, just a little over an hour from Salinas, and I had nothing to lose. Besides, I had my brother watching in the stands and friends from high school and college. On the day of the race as I'm about to get into my blocks, I can hear friends calling my name. I'm just thinking, "Whatever happens, happens. No one expects anything anyway." We get up in the set position and the gun goes off. I'm running right along with everyone else at the first turn. I think, "OK, I can run with these guys." We're now on the backstretch and at 200 meters I hear one of my friends call my name. I'm even seeing some of my friends in the stands. I was so inexperienced that I really wasn't even concentrating. At the top of the turn, 300 meters, I'm in fifth position. As we come off the turn toward the homestretch I'm still full of energy. So I push and I start to pass one guy after another. At 40 meters I catch Darnell Hall, who was a big name internationally in the 400 meters. No one was really close to Michael Johnson but Darnell was the closest. I go right past Darnell and hold on all the way through the finish line. The crowd is going crazy, my coach is going nuts, my brother is screaming and yelling. It felt good to be a winner. I went 45.12, my personal record to that point. That time qualified me for the Olympic Trials. I signed on with Nike, too. The dream was on.

CALVIN

As we prepared to leave Salinas for Atlanta and the trials, I remember feeling completely confident in my ability to make the team. I knew I had done everything necessary to prepare for that moment. I did all the work and it showed in the events I ran leading up to the trials. Once we got to Atlanta the feeling was even stronger. I knew we were supposed to be there. We were living our destiny and all we had to do was exactly what we had been doing for six months. The first two rounds of the 400 meters went great for Alvin and me. We moved through them without a problem and both of us qualified for the semifinals. Alvin ran in the first heat on the third day. By the time I left the tent, I knew he had qualified for the finals. All I had to do was my end. I knew that if I made it to the finals, I would make the U.S. Team. But early in my semifinal heat I lost my rhythm. I became overanxious and instead of calming myself down and focusing on my race, I started to run someone else's race. I was able to hold on but I crossed the finish line in a photo finish with Jason Rouser. When they flashed the results on the stadium's big screen, they showed Jason had finished 7/1000ths of a second ahead of me for the fourth and final spot in the finals. I remember feeling devastated. Alvin and I had started this journey and now my brother would be on his own while I watched him from home.

ALVIN

I knew it was up to me to represent everything we had done to that point. When I arrived at the track the next day I realized there was no turning back. I thought about everything we had been through, all the people that doubted us. I thought about the Mustang, the bad jobs, the long hours alone with my coach on the track. It was like my entire life was passing before my eyes and I had the chance to change everything that had come before in one race. I knew I could run with these guys. The top six in the finals qualified for the Olympic Team with the top three qualifying for the open 400 meters. The race turned out to be a blur. I shot out of the blocks and after about 200 meters it looked like the race belonged to Michael Johnson and me. Then, out of nowhere, I saw Butch Reynolds, whose world record Michael broke, with his long arms and legs. Butch passed

me with about 75 meters to go but I held on and finished third. It took two world record holders using all they had to beat me that day. I ran 44.07, the fastest I had ever run in my life.

CALVIN

I wanted to be a part of the show so bad that it made me sick. Even after the trials I was hoping somebody would drop out and that I would get another chance. But it never came. All I could do was live the whole experience through Alvin. I went home to Salinas and back to the apartment with Marie.

ALVIN

Every athlete who makes the United States Olympic Team gets processed a few weeks before the Games. I had no idea what making the Olympic Team would mean to us long term and I certainly didn't expect all the benefits that came right away. We were fitting for the clothes we'd wear at the opening and closing ceremonies. They took measurements for casual clothes we could wear around the Olympic Village. They sized our fingers for the Olympic ring every athlete received and they measured our feet for new shoes. We got pagers, cell phones, all kinds of high-end stuff. And they gave us tickets for the Games for our family. It was like no Christmas I had ever had. It was fun, but I was going through all of this while Calvin was on the outside looking in. I was balancing my excitement against his absence, which kind of evened out my emotions.

When I walked into the Olympic Village in Atlanta for the first time, all I thought about was the race. Even to that point I really didn't have much experience and now I was going to run four days in a row, if I was lucky, against the greatest 400-meter runners in the world. At just every moment I was trying to see the race in my mind. I had never run before the number of people who would be there every day. I was scared just because that was the most immediate emotion when you realize where you are and what you have to do to be successful. There was no way I could go into that environment completely confident. Even the greatest athlete in the world feels a sense of intensity and anxiety going into an Olympic race.

It would be just like the trials for me. I would get on the track and run scared just as I had through four rounds a few weeks earlier. When I'm in good shape I, never know how fast I'm running. In the end, I became the first person to ever run under 45 seconds in the 400 meters in all four rounds of the Olympics.

The night before the finals I couldn't sleep at all. I was using visual imaging to play the race over and over in my mind. I knew my lane assignment and I knew where all the other guys would be on the track. I had run fast for three days in a row. But I had never imagined the size of the crowd or the intensity of the atmosphere inside the stadium. It literally looked like a sea of people and I realized they were there to see us run. The race took place at night and it was lightning and thundering as we walked onto the track. The thunder rumbled through the stadium and it started to drizzle, which actually made me calmer. It was like I felt comfortable with nature entering the scene. I tried to absorb the moment and take in everything I could see. I heard a couple of people calling my name and I looked around at what seemed like a thousand cameras. I don't know if those minutes went by fast or slow, but I remember hearing the command "Sweats off." I could feel my heart pumping and my chest moving. I kept telling myself, "Power and acceleration from the beginning to the end." I repeated those words over and over as I headed to the blocks. Blood was flowing all through my body. I was trying to calm down and I remember what my brother had said about running down the backstretch: "Float like a butterfly, float like a butterfly." I was able to calm myself until the command to get into the set position. After that, my mind went blank. I didn't hear anything and I didn't see anything. Pow! The gun goes off and I explode. I'm thinking about maintaining my rhythm and running my race until I get around the first curve.

Everybody's running as hard as they can so I just take off. I'm running with the pack and I'm in great position. As we come to the homestretch Roger Black, from England, passes me at the 320-meter mark and then Davis Kamoga, from Uganda, passes me at 350 meters and holds me off at the finish line. I finish fourth, just a fraction of a second out of the medals.

C A L V I N

I was in the stands watching and I saw every step Alvin took. I knew exactly what he was thinking. I knew how he felt and I could feel my own heart pounding as Alvin ran around the track. Most of all, I knew how he felt when he looked up at that huge screen and saw he had finished fourth. The security was extremely tight in Atlanta so I couldn't get down onto the track to see Alvin. We were able to spend some time together later that night but Alvin still had a race to run. The 4 x 400-meter relay would be his chance for a gold medal but I had to go back to Salinas. Alvin only had enough tickets for our father, mother and grandmother. I would watch from the couch inside the Heather Circle apartment complex with my eyes full of tears. I tried not to cry when Alvin took the baton on the second leg of the relay and carried the U.S. to a four-meter lead. But how could I hold back those tears? We had made it to the Olympic Games less than a year after we had made it out of an old Mustang on a hill in Northern California. It might have been Alvin inside that television, but it was me, too.

A L V I N

All I remember was a sense of relief. The pressure was off. We had done the impossible, even if it was only me down there on the track in Atlanta. The whole world knew about Alvin and Calvin Harrison after the 1996 Olympics. We had become *somebody*. We had a name and we were known as some of the best athletes on the planet. The Olympic experience had painted a new picture. It was like we had a new beginning.

C A L V I N

I had the same feeling Alvin had when he saw me run the 400 meters. I watched him win a gold medal in the Olympic Games and that gave me confidence I could win an Olympic gold medal too. Everything looked promising. I knew we could do whatever we wanted in track and field. And I knew track and field represented our destiny.

NO ONE HAS EVER RUN

THE 400 METERS LIKE MICHAEL JOHNSON

HE FINISHED FIRST and I finished second in the 400-meter finals at the 2000 Olympics in Sydney. Michael beat me by three or four meters. He finished in 43.83 and I ran 44.40. The funny thing about the 400 meters is that the faster you run the less tired you are after the race. The more relaxed and efficiently you run, the faster you go and the less fatigue you feel. **ALVIN**

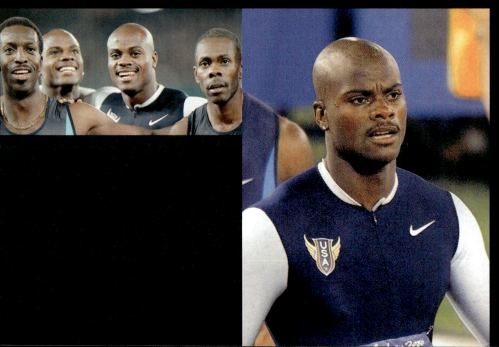

Alvin ran the third leg and passed the baton to me for the anchor. Since I missed the 1996 Games, I dreamed of two things: Running with Michael Johnson, which I did in the finals at Sydney, and either handing off or receiving the baton from my brother in the 4 x 400-meter relay. **CALVIN**

REALIZE OUR DREAM

I'M RECEIVING the stick from Antonio Pettigrew in the finals of the 4 x 400-meter relay in Sydney. All I'm thinking about is doing my part. I want to give Michael (Johnson) a nice lead for the final leg and I'm hoping to run fast enough to give us a chance at the world record. Everything I had worked for in my career came together as I took the baton. I was ready. **CALVIN**

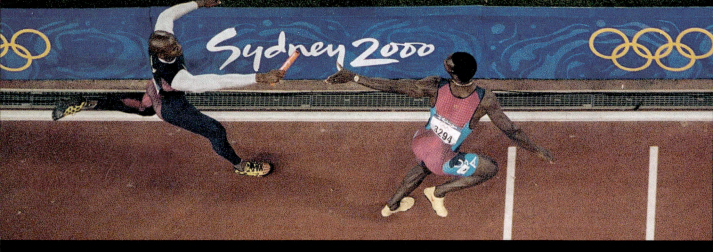

TOP OF THE MOUNTAIN

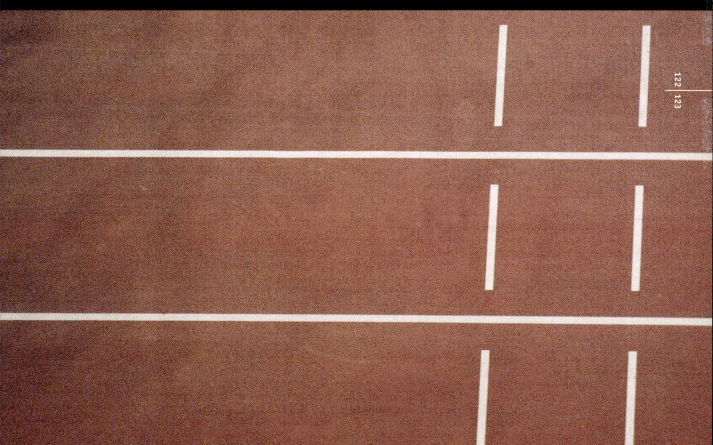

I'M HANDING THE BATON to Michael Johnson for the final leg of the 4 x 400-meter finals in Sydney. I gave Michael a comfortable lead and he brought it home. Alvin won his second gold medal and I won my first. Now that I look back, I will be the last guy to have handed the stick to Michael Johnson in the Olympics. **CALVIN**

I'VE DONE MY JOB in the finals. Now it's up to Michael Johnson, and we all knew no one would catch him. Antonio Pettigrew, Alvin, me and Michael show off the gold. **CALVIN**

ALL SIX MEMBERS of the 2000 400-meter United States Olympic Team after the 4 x 400-meter relay final. From left to right, Angelo Taylor, who won the gold medal in the 400-meter hurdles, Antonio Pettigrew, Jerome Young, Calvin and me hugging Michael on our victory lap. **ALVIN**

the fact that we have just begun to understand what we're doing on the track. I think we can become the fastest humans on the planet in the 200 and 400 meters over the next four years. Before long it could be Calvin and me running against each other with everyone else trying to catch up. **ALVIN**

5

BACK IN THE SHADOWS AGAIN

ALVIN

We were like conquering heroes when I returned to Salinas from Atlanta. It seemed like Calvin and I could go anywhere and people we had never seen before recognized us and wanted to talk about the Olympics. Everybody wanted to see the gold medal. We did radio shows, television shows and interviews for the local newspapers. The whole city seemed to embrace us. Given where we had been and what Salinas had meant to our lives at that point, the warmth was comforting. We were two guys that had great success at the high school level, returned to live in a car and against even our coaches' advice decided to take a run at the Olympic Games. We literally came out of nowhere. We had done what most considered to be the impossible in one of the hardest events in track and field.

We had no idea what was just around the corner. Just like that mountain we climbed at Arroyo Seco, Calvin and I thought we knew what we'd find at the top. What we found out after the 1996 Olympics was that not only did we not get to the top, but all the steps still ahead of us would present a challenge that we couldn't see coming.

CALVIN

Alvin and I had a Jeep that we had parked in the same spot for a year inside the apartment complex where we all lived. One day right after we returned to Salinas, I walked out of my apartment and saw this guy towing our Jeep away. I saw the name of the place on the truck and called the guy. He obviously knew who we were from the Olympics and he probably thought Alvin had become a millionaire or something. He said it would cost us $300 to get the Jeep back and there was nothing we could do about it. The guy had been doing this scam for months and we were the perfect target. I'm sure he figured we would just pay the money and keep the whole thing quiet. When we hung up, Alvin and I went to get our Jeep. We weren't about to pay this guy $300. There was a gate at the front of the tow yard and I started pushing the gate open. Another guy comes out and is trying to push the gate closed but he's not strong enough. We get through the gate, jump in the Jeep and start to drive it back home. Meanwhile, the guy who owns the place is trying to get Alvin to fight him. He's yelling and saying, "I know who you guys are. I'll sue you." Alvin just kept his arms straight up in the air because we knew that guy would take a punch in exchange for a few thousand

dollars. Eventually Alvin jumped into the Jeep and we drove back to our apartment. Neither one of us felt like we had done a thing wrong. After all we had been through and to come back and have somebody trying to take advantage of our success, it was too much.

A L V I N

I felt violated by somebody who was obviously used to violating defenseless people. If you live in an apartment and don't have the newest car, there is a good chance you can't afford to have your only means of transportation taken away. I'm sure most of these people just paid the $300 to avoid a fight they didn't think they could win. I couldn't do that. The guy had called the police by the time we returned home. He tells the police I grabbed him by his head, slammed him into the hood of the Jeep, threw him to the ground and kicked him. The police come to our apartment and it's pretty clear they believe the guy so they arrest me. Calvin was so upset seeing me in handcuffs that he grabbed them. I said, "Don't worry, Calvin, everything's going to be all right." The next thing I know Calvin's getting arrested, too, and we're off to the police station. We get downtown and they start interrogating us like we're on television. It was so dramatic. I'm sure it was because of all the publicity about us. Finally, a woman who had been across the street from the tow yard came down to the police station. She saw the whole thing and provided a statement that supported everything Calvin and I were saying. After that the policemen knew the guy was lying. Then all kinds of people started coming forward because the guy had been towing legally parked cars for years. The business eventually was shut down.

A L V I N

After every major meet Calvin and I returned home to spend time with our family in Florida. In 1996, we didn't get back to Orlando until about six weeks after the Olympics. My little sister, Africia, was living with my dad at the time and she had a 2-year-old son, Shaddrick. We talked to Africia about coming to California and getting a fresh start. We knew what her living conditions were and we knew how life in Orlando could steal your spirit. She was a beautiful girl that just needed to find her own way in the world. Calvin and I told Africia we would take Shaddrick back to California with us while she cleaned up her affairs and prepared to come west. I told Africia I would send her a plane ticket as soon as some money I was expecting arrived. We agreed she would leave in a little over a week.

Unfortunately, the money didn't arrive as soon as I had hoped. Calvin and I were taking care of Shaddrick, but it would be a few more days before I could buy a plane ticket to California. Africia called me on the day we originally set for her departure from someplace in Jacksonville. I told her I was still working on the ticket, but that everything would be fine. I remember asking her what she was doing in Jacksonville. She told me she was hanging out with this "crazy guy," but that she was going to ask him to take her home. I told her I loved her and then spoke the last words my little sister would ever hear from me: "Be careful."

That night I didn't sleep comfortably. At around 1 a.m. I suddenly had shortness of breath. It was like I could feel the breath of life leaving my body. I was familiar enough with these feelings that I thought I was about to die. I felt like I was winded and I needed to catch my breath to stay alive. Immediately I started praying to God and asking Him not to take me. At that moment I thought it was my time to die. What I didn't know was that I was feeling the breath of life being taken away from my sister. The next thing I know the phone is ringing and it's 3 a.m. It's my dad. He has this raspy kind of older man's voice. He says, "Son, this is your daddy. Your sister has been murdered. She was shot and killed." I couldn't believe what I was hearing. I kept asking my father if he was sure they had the right person. I just knew it was a case of mistaken identity. He said, "Son, it is your sister. Tell your brother." I couldn't absorb what I was hearing. It was impossible for me to believe what was happening. I had just talked to her.

The guy shot her in the back seven times and she fell through a sliding-glass door trying to get away. He killed her with another couple in the living room of the guy's parent's house. The guy's parents were in their bedroom down the hallway when all this took place. They had been arguing when he ran out to his car. There were a lot of people who saw him go to the car and pull the .45 from beneath the seat. He went back in the house and he started to unload. The next day his friends turned him in. Later, after the reality of her death sunk in, I realized I had seen it all happen in a vision. I saw bullets flying and I thought Calvin was the one being shot. I could see seven bullets, and as they flew toward us I kept pulling Calvin out of the way. But it was her. My little sister was shot seven times in the back. My mind was racing with thoughts. I felt guilty because I hadn't been able to get her onto a plane that night. I saw the entire thing before it happened and I did nothing to stop it. I wondered what might have happened if I had had the ticket. Would she have asked the guy to take her home earlier? I already had mixed emotions about the Olympics because Calvin hadn't been a part of the success. Now I was crushed. I felt devastated. I just wanted to quit everything.

C A L V I N

I asked all the questions, but I never found any answers. Why did this happen to someone so young and beautiful? What could I have done to save her? Though I hurt down to my bones, Alvin and I dealt with her death differently. I was able to compartmentalize my life and emotions and still go to the track. Alvin couldn't escape the memory. I never considered the option of no longer running. I was devastated. But I never allowed those feelings to run over onto the track. They were two separate issues for me.

Through it all we never considered stopping running. It's what we do. Of course, our sister's murder was devastating. I don't ever think it influenced me to give up track. I asked questions as to why it happened. But I never asked those questions in the context of track and field because those were two separate issues. When I was alone, I would meditate and talk to God about what had happened and try to understand and deal with my emotions. But for me at least, the track became a refuge, a place I could come and work through the pain.

A L V I N

I responded differently to Africia's death. I was the last person in our family she talked to on the day of her murder. I felt so much guilt that I lost motivation. I kept wondering what I could have done to change that day. I kept thinking about the lifestyle I was living in California, which was a little bit better than the lifestyle she had in Florida. I had her son right there in bed with me every night. I couldn't

separate her death from my performance on the track. They were parts of the same life and I couldn't find a way to pull them apart.

C A L V I N

I finally came to see death, even an awful death of someone you love, as a part of life. I knew I couldn't dwell on the darkness of it all for too much longer because I still had a life to live and she would have wanted me to follow my destiny. It was just something I had to get over the best I could. I loved her, but I had to move on to save myself.

A L V I N

I practiced and entered meets but I just wasn't motivated. I didn't run well at all in 1997. It was like I was out of it for the entire year. I destroyed my apartment the night I got the news of my little sister's death and Calvin did the same thing. We had to pay extra money to fix the places up when we moved out a few months later. Neither one of us wanted to send Shaddrick back to Florida because that's where his mother had died. He was so small and innocent that we thought he should stay with us in California. Our parents eventually convinced us to send him back to Florida, but we didn't go back for the funeral. We couldn't bear the thought of seeing our little sister like that. We wanted to remember her just the way we had seen her when we left Florida. She had been smiling and waving as we pulled away and that was the image we wanted to hang on to. Just about everybody in the family was upset with us but we didn't care. If I had been in a prize fight my sister's death would have been one of those blows that knocked me to the canvass. I never saw it coming and for a while all I could do was hang on.

A L V I N

The year between the fall of 1996 and the fall of 1997 just wasn't a good time for us. There seemed to be so many distractions in our personal lives and we were still dealing with our sister's death. We had made a big enough name for ourselves that we didn't have to keep a job. Our Nike contract allowed us to train and run the international circuit. I felt like we were being bombarded by a constant flow of issues that we had to deal with. We weren't without fault. We had gone from living in a car to the Olympics in 12 months and

suddenly we were expected to understand all the nuances of a normal life. In fact, we still had a lot to learn about things most people take for granted. It seemed like we spent that entire year of 1997 cleaning up our lives and clearing our minds.

C A L V I N

As disappointing as that time was it also rejuvenated us. We dealt with our sister's death, refocused our attention on the goals and objectives we had set out for ourselves and slowly started to improve. By the time the National Indoor Track and Field Championships rolled around in early 1998, we were back on our game. Alvin took first and I took second in the 400 meters with the third and fourth fastest indoor times in the history of the 400 meters. Only two people, Michael Johnson and Danny Everett, had ever run faster indoors than Alvin and I did in Atlanta in 1998. Alvin went 45.05 and I ran 45.18. We were back.

A L V I N

We went to Greece for the Athena Indoor meet in Pireaus and we broke the meet record there, too. Then we went to South Africa and ran the fastest 400 meters ever recorded outdoor in that country. I ran 44.26 and Calvin ran 44.68 to break the mark of 44.72.

C A L V I N

With the World Championships coming up that summer, I knew Alvin and I were ready. We had regained our confidence and our times were some of the fastest in the world that year. We went down to Indianapolis for the U.S. Nationals, which would determine the United States team for the World Championships. The back of my left knee had been bothering me right around the peroneal nerve, which runs from the back of the knee down into the foot. As Alvin and I rested in our hotel room the night before the first round of the 400 meters, I decided to ice the back of my knee in hopes of completely eliminating the pain. I iced the area for about 35 minutes, which is about 15 or 20 minutes longer than usual. I knew I had iced it a little too long but I didn't want to feel anything when I went to the track the next morning. What I didn't know is that the ice made the

nerve constrict to the point that it just shut down, causing a temporary paralysis of my left foot. The doctors called it "drop foot syndrome" and I couldn't move the foot up and down. My foot just hung there like it was dead. I had just finished icing when I started to stand up. I took one step and nearly fell to the floor because my foot wouldn't work. I said to Alvin, "Did you see that? I think something's wrong with my leg." Alvin told me not to worry and that it happens all the time. I knew he was right. I figured once the knee thawed out the feeling in my foot would come back. As the hours pass nothing is happening. I'm starting to get worried, but Alvin keeps telling me everything will be fine in the morning.

A L V I N

I'm lying on the other bed confident the feeling will be back by the time we wake up. We were always icing one part of our body or another and I had experienced that dead feeling before too. But the feeling always came back so I didn't think this time would be any different.

CALVIN

I went to sleep thinking the feeling would come back. Deep down I had no doubt I'd wake up and be fine. During the course of the night I noticed the foot was still numb, but I didn't think too much of it. Then I wake up to go to the bathroom and as I get out of bed I nearly fall down again. Still, I'm telling myself everything is fine. The feeling will come back. Now it's time to get up for the day. I just lay in the bed for a few minutes thinking. I knew only a few hours had passed since I last tried to walk. I'm a little scared, but I swing my feet over the side of the bed and stand up. The same thing happens again and I almost go down. Now I know I'm in trouble. I called Coach Shaw to let him know what was going on.

ALVIN

Coach Shaw came into the room and he knew what had happened. He had called the doctors and they were pretty sure about the diagnosis. I could see it in Coach Shaw's eyes. He didn't know what to say because Calvin just broke down crying. He couldn't feel a thing in that foot.

CALVIN

The doctors tried everything. They did pressure therapy. They used electronic stimulation. They tried accupressure to different points along my leg. The doctor finally tells me that he's had these cases before with NFL athletes and that it takes eight months or longer to heal. That's when it hit me. I could be out for up to a year. I went back to the hotel room and broke down. I had just missed making the Olympic Team in 1996, I had a horrible 1997 and here I was having a great year leading up to the qualifying meet for the World Championships. I felt like that whole world had turned its back on me. If I was ever going to give up, this was the point.

ALVIN

It was just like 1996 all over again. I didn't know if Calvin's career was over or not, but I couldn't let his injury stop us. I assumed the big-brother role. I would take care of both of us if that's what it took. Even if it turned out to be a career-ending injury, we were going to find a way to do something special together. I didn't know if Calvin would end up training me or what, but I was not going to allow that injury to slow us down. If

I had to do all the running, fine. We had come too far to let an injury slow us down. I was going to run for both of us.

CALVIN

It took at least eight months before I could get back on the track and run. I was doing three or four hours of therapy up to four times a week. I was most scared the first couple weeks when nothing was happening. After about two months I could feel tiny impulses in my foot. I was holding on to whatever positive feedback I could find. It wasn't until February or March of 1999 that I could run anywhere close to the way I had been running before the injury. I ran maybe two meets the entire calendar year of 1999 because I was so timid once I got back on the track. I had a lot of self-doubt as to my ability to get back into my previous form. Eventually I realized I had to look forward, not backward. I did not want my career to end with that injury. I wanted to prove to everyone, including myself, that I could still run fast.

ALVIN

You have to understand that Calvin's inside foot was essentially paralyzed. That's the leg you push off on as you round the corners in the 400 meters. To some extent that foot has to be stronger than the other one. If he had tried to run before the injury completely healed, he might have broken his leg.

CALVIN

It wasn't until around May of 1999 that I felt completely comfortable on the track. The nationals were coming around again, but I didn't feel confident enough in my ability to run any races of consequence. Alvin was fighting groin and knee injuries that season, so it was turning into another year of recovery for both of us. Mentally I was trying to convince myself I could still compete on the international circuit. I had lost quality time and I felt like I had been left behind by the pack. I didn't want to enter races only to be beaten week after week and humiliated. I decided to do all my training alone.

Had we known exactly what was ahead of us after our success in 1996, I'm not sure we would have found the strength to continue to move ahead. But we managed to keep putting one foot in front of the other just as we had done since childhood.

Early in 1999, I put my family in the car and drove to Orlando. I knew my grandmother wasn't doing well and I wanted my children to see her. We stayed for a few days and everyone had a good time. I think seeing all of us brought some joy to our grandmother. Toward the end of our stay we were all sitting on my grandmother's bed and the kids were in the room playing. Pretty soon everyone left except me. She looked at me and told me she had a story to tell me. She said, "Alvin, there was this man and he had a mother who was ailing. She was sick and on her deathbed. So the family called the man and told him his mother was about to pass. The man got into his car and started driving. He was in Georgia and his mother was in Florida. He was speeding like crazy and a cop pulled him over. The cop said, 'Do you know how fast you were going? Why are you speeding?' The man said, 'Officer, I know I was going fast. I know I was speeding but my mother is on her death bed. I don't know how much time she has

left. I have to get to her before she goes.' The cop says, 'OK, I want you to follow behind me and I'm going to escort you through the state.' He turned on his lights and escorted the man all the way through the state of Georgia. The man made it to his mother and was able to see her before she passed." Now my grandmother is telling me this story and in my head I'm thinking, "Where's grandma going with this?" It wasn't until afterward that I understood she knew her time was coming. She was getting ready to go. I knew what she was telling me. Shortly after that, just a couple days, I felt her spirit come into me. It was like the strength she had to keep the family together was being passed on to someone else now. I felt that spirit come into me.

Not long after I returned to California, Calvin and I headed to San Diego for a two-month training camp. We had just arrived there when we received the call. The doctors told our family my grandmother had 24 hours to live. They said she wouldn't make it through the next day. I knew we had to get to her immediately. But a round-trip ticket from San Diego to Orlando was around $2,000 apiece. We went to our room and started to pray. I had no idea how we would find the money to buy a ticket, but I knew we had to get there.

CALVIN

We talked to Dixon Farmer, who was a coach and director at the camp. Since United Airlines was an Olympic sponsor at the time, Dixon called them and was able to work something out where we got tickets for $300 apiece. We left the next day and arrived in Orlando around 11 o'clock Wednesday night. Alvin and I went directly to the hospital and stayed there until about noon the next day. The only time we left was to grab something to eat early Thursday afternoon. We came right back and we were there when she passed.

ALVIN

She hung on the whole time Calvin and I worked on the plane tickets. When we finally arrived in Orlando she was lying in the bed and not moving at all. Her eyes were wide open and they wouldn't blink. We had to keep putting water on this big cotton swab to keep her mouth moist. Everyone kept telling her that Alvin and Calvin were there and we kept talking to her so she could hear our voices. The only sign she gave that she knew we were there came when she blinked her eye. A single tear rolled down the side of her face. We knew she wanted to say something. Her mind was still there but her body had just given out at that point. She wanted to hug us. We could feel it. When we arrived the heart monitor machine was so slow, because she was barely alive. One reason we know she knew we were there is that her heart rate went way up when we came into the room. Our grandmother had two sons of her own. At the time, one of them was in jail and the other one was in prison. All she wanted was to see both of her sons together before she passed. The one in jail was able to be released long enough to see her before she passed. The other one wasn't able to leave prison. I believe God intended for us to be her sons. And we were there by her side.

CALVIN

When she passed we were on either side of her holding her hands and praying. I could feel it the moment she passed. I could feel her spirit leaving her body. Our relationship with her had grown so much at the spiritual level that we continued to have a telepathic kind of relationship even from California.

She couldn't speak out loud, but she spoke to me right before she passed. I could feel her telling me, "Alvin, don't cry. I know you want to cry but you need to be strong for the rest of them. If they see you cry they will break down." I wanted to cry, but I had to hold it in. We were closer to my grandmother than her own children. It would be fair to say she was our mother. As a matter of fact, that's what our biological mother told us, "That's your mother right there. She raised you and that's your momma right there." When my grandmother was alive you could always tell our mother was uncomfortable with how close we were to our grandmother. She died in 1999 and her voice is still on the answering machine at my father's house. Sometimes, and I know Calvin does this too, I'll call the house just to hear her voice. The sound of her voice provides a sense of comfort. I do that at least once a week.

It was as if a great force had been removed from my life. There was this hole that nothing could fill. At the same time I knew she had gone in peace. Before Alvin and I arrived in Orlando, she had told everyone not to worry because she was going home. I knew we had to stay strong because that's what she wanted from Alvin and me. We knew her passing was part of life, but it was still a major loss. From the time we were old enough to use a telephone, we would call my grandmother with any positive news about our lives. It could have been a fashion show we were in as high school freshmen, a good grade on a test, a successful track meet or just something special to us. We would call her every single time because we knew our success made her happy. Once she passed I knew those phone calls were over. The little kiss on the forehead, the "hickey" as she called it, had been the one constant of our childhood. When Alvin and I went to California, conversation became our connection. There was no one else of her stature in our lives. She had raised us and we wanted to show her that we had listened and that we were doing the things she had taught us to become someone. So much of what Alvin and I had become was because of how she had nurtured us. It was like we were starting to bloom and we wanted to be sure she knew all her love and guidance was paying off.

ALVIN

Calvin and I went back home to Salinas to train for the U.S. Nationals. Neither one of us were running particularly well. Calvin was still dealing with the injury to his foot and I wasn't as consistent as I would have liked. But I got to the nationals and blazed through the first two rounds. In the finals I explode out of my blocks for the first four steps. I'm feeling great and then cramps attack my calves. Now I can't run on my toes so I finish the race running flat footed. I couldn't push off my toes to gain power and momentum. I finished dead last. It seemed like a fitting conclusion to what seemed like one problem after another.

CALVIN

I was just trying to heal mentally and physically at that point from everything we had gone through. I wasn't ready to give up but I didn't know exactly what I needed to do to succeed either. I didn't how to make the situation right. I was questioning everything I was doing and trying to figure out how to get myself back. I was still doing light therapy at the time and I wasn't sure about much of anything on the track. Could I run as fast as I did before? Will I be able to regain enough confidence to prepare myself for 2000?

ALVIN

We decided to move back to Florida and train with Brooks Johnson, who had coached Butch Reynolds. Butch had the world record in the 400 meters before Michael Johnson set the new record of 43.18. We had known Brooks since high school and we knew he understood what we needed to get to the next level. Brooks had not only trained a world record holder, but he trained a guy who set the record in our event. It was like we knew we were doing some things wrong but just weren't sure what they were. We worked out at Walt Disney World's Wide World of Sports complex on a competition track and Brooks seemed like the perfect guy. As it turned out he was the perfect guy – for Calvin.

CALVIN

We were staying at a luxury apartment in an area around Orlando called Metro West. This was big-time living for us. We never knew anybody that lived at Metro West when we grew up. Lennox Boulevard was actually right down the street, four or five miles from the Carlyle Apartments in Metro West. But it might as well have been four or five hundred away. It didn't seem that long ago that we were living in shack of a house on Lennox and Aaron Avenue and here we were living in a place that represented the high life.

ALVIN

I remember thinking, "This is our home, Orlando. But look at us now." When Calvin and I left Orlando we were broomstick skinny. Here we were grown up fit and strong. It made me feel like we had accomplished something in life. We had made progress in our lives. There was still a lot to be done, but we weren't going back to that house on Lennox Boulevard. Being in that apartment was something I wanted my grandmother to see. I wished I could have brought her over, cooked her dinner, massaged her shoulders and talked about all the things we had done and were about to do.

CALVIN

Once I started training it seemed like I had to learn everything all over again. I was even intimidated by the workouts at first. I slowly started to come around to the point that I couldn't wait for the next session. Brooks would explain the reason behind everything we did. He would break down our technique and form so we could understand the logic behind the process. It was like Brooks was breaking us down so he could build us back up in a way that would make us better. He's an excellent coach, but he's an even better teacher. I tried to absorb everything he said and incorporate it into my approach on and off the track. At the time, I needed Brooks. I was trying to regain my confidence so I could compete with the fastest people on earth. He was stern and right to the point. If I was doing well, he would let me know. If I wasn't doing something right, he let me know that too. There wasn't a lot of gray area with Brooks. I needed that direction because it was encouraging. I knew he knew what he was talking about.

ALVIN

One of the differences between Calvin and me is how we adjust to change. When our father first called us to go out to California when we were kids, Calvin was the one who stayed. I'm more emotional so I needed to go back home and slowly get used to the idea of leaving everything I knew. To some extent it was the same when my little sister was killed. Calvin dealt with the grief more pragmatically. He could separate his personal life from his professional life. For me, it all runs together. I enjoyed working with Brooks and I could see Calvin improving. But I didn't feel comfortable. I kept thinking about Salinas and how comfortable I felt on that track at Hartnell. I was used to going to the track every day and seeing people running around while I trained. They knew who I was and they offered encouragement. I fed off that interaction. I needed that connection. It motivated me and I felt a sense of support. The Disney track was inside a huge facility. Calvin and I would be training with Brooks all by ourselves. I knew I needed to get back to the place that had become my home. One day, December 31, 1999, I just woke up and knew I had to get up and go. I had been hearing this voice in my head telling me to get back to California. I went to the bus station, bought a ticket and headed back. I didn't see any fireworks and I didn't kiss anybody when the clock struck midnight. For four days I rode that bus. I told Calvin, "If I stay in Florida, I won't make the 2000 Olympic Team." I needed to go.

CALVIN

I needed exactly what Florida offered at that time. Alvin hadn't experienced what I had experienced the last eight months. I needed to be motivated again. I had to understand what I needed to do on the track and why I needed to do it. I didn't start to get my confidence back until February or March when I won a couple of races at meets in Florida. In track and field, all the work you do in December and January doesn't catch up with you until February and March. I was seeing the results of all my hard work and slowly regaining my confidence. I knew the Olympic Trials were right in our backyard in Sacramento and I felt like I was going to be ready.

ALVIN

We were not going to fail in front of our people and that's how we looked at the trials. The fact that we would be performing in front of people who had watched us since high school motivated Calvin and me. I knew we would make the 2000 Olympic Team.

CALVIN

I counted down the days to the Olympics on my calendar. Every day I would tell Alvin, "Only 50 more days. We're one day closer. Remember when it was 250 days?" After the trials were over and we made the team it really didn't hit me until I went down to San Diego to get processed. All the things Alvin had told me about Atlanta in 1996 I experienced. They measured us for everything, the Olympic ring, shoes, belts, pants, shirts. They gave us a leather Olympic jacket and decals to put on our cars. I was officially a member of the United States Olympic Team. I remember feeling so proud to be representing the United States.

ALVIN

I was most excited for Calvin. I would be going to the Olympic Games with my brother. Not another track and field athlete in the history of the Olympic Games could say that. We were about to make history.

9

GOLD FUTURES

ALVIN

Australia was more of a spiritual celebration for me because I was with my brother. I didn't feel as overwhelmed as I did when I left for Atlanta. We had survived tragedy, death and injury just to put ourselves in a position to compete in Sydney. As we boarded the flight to Australia I couldn't help but look over at Calvin. How many times had we crossed the country between California and Florida? How many lessons had we learned together? How many times had we shared a laugh? How many times had his tears been my tears? We spent days in buses getting from one side of America to the other in search of our lives. We lived in the same Mustang that carried us back to California at a time when all we knew was that we had to leave Florida. We struggled with the basic questions of life at the same time we dreamed of the Olympic Games. As I looked at Calvin I saw myself. Yet there were no scars. Somehow we had made it through the twisted corners of our lives without permanent damage. The basic lessons of good and bad, right and wrong, taught to us by our grandmother had not been lost amid the battle to define ourselves. We had learned how to put one foot in front of the other. Ironically, the speed at which we were now capable of doing so landed us on an airplane headed to a world stage.

We had become the first brothers ever to make an Olympic Team together. At the same time, I knew that anything could happen. If the past four years taught us anything, it was that we had to be prepared for things we couldn't even imagine. I knew what it felt like to think everything was going fine only to be hit with something that I never saw coming. I was excited about going to Australia, but I was humble, too. I was so used to expecting the unexpected that I don't think I was capable of being too excited. I was content, but very aware of every moment. It was my way of protecting myself.

Still, walking into that stadium in Sydney for the first time was magnificent. I was calmer than Calvin because I had experienced the opening ceremony in Atlanta. But that stadium was stunning. Every aspect of that place was beautiful.

C A L V I N

There were more than 120,000 people there for the opening ceremony, but it looked like there were millions. We were coming through the tunnel and screaming just like we were about to play a football game. Every one of us knew exactly what the other one was feeling. We had worked the entire year to get

to that moment and no one could contain their excitement. It was a dream coming true. I think I lost my voice that night yelling in sheer joy. It was so beautiful and the roar of the crowd was unbelievable. I stood on the track trying to absorb everything I saw. I remember thinking that I never wanted to forget that moment.

If all went well, I knew I would have the chance to run on that track with Michael Johnson in the finals of the 4 x 400-meter relay. And I knew I would run a relay on that same surface in the Olympic Games with my brother. The whole experience was exhilarating. It was like I was telling myself to hold on tight because I was going on a joy ride.

A L V I N

Calvin and I spent nearly three weeks training and traveling around Australia before we checked into the Olympic Village. The difference between Atlanta and Sydney is that we understood the road we were on and we knew where it was taking us so we weren't going to be surprised by the outcome. When I went to Atlanta in 1996 I didn't know what to expect. I didn't know how I would feel running in front of that kind of crowd. I didn't know the competition very well because that was my first year running the 400 meters. In 2000 I knew the runners, their strengths and weaknesses, and I knew myself and what I could accomplish. In 1996 I was just running scared. In 2000, I was running to win.

By the time we checked into the Olympic Village, we were ready to go. The coaches gave us the heat sheets for the 400 meters a few days ahead of the first round. Every 400-meter runner was listed with his best time of the year. I knew I could get into the finals and I knew I could be in the top three. But I was in such good shape that I didn't know how fast I was running in the early rounds. Calvin and I had never trained under world-class conditions until we worked with Brooks Johnson. So we didn't know what it felt like to be in perfect condition at exactly the right moment. It was an advantage and a disadvantage.

CALVIN

Alvin ran 44.25 in the second round and he shut it down with 100 meters to go. Now he's my brother and I've seen him do a lot of things, but he never wowed me like that before. When they showed his time on the big screen, I couldn't believe what he had done. And that was running hard for only 75 percent of the race. If he hadn't shut it down to conserve energy for the next round, he would have run somewhere between 43.50 and 43.80.

ALVIN

The night of the 400-meter finals I arrived at the track with Bubba Thornton, the coach of the men's team, and my brother. They were taking me through the race and telling me things I already knew but that I needed to keep fresh in my mind. I made my way out to the track and looked for Michael Johnson, who was out a little earlier than normal. I knew I could beat Michael that night. I knew I was going to win. Michael knew I could match his strength because I had run the first three rounds in less than 45 seconds. The fact that he knew what I was capable of doing gave me even more confidence. Now it was all about the lane assignments. I was in Lane 4 and he was in Lane 6. Until the finals I had run in Lane 6 so I had become comfortable there. But I couldn't think about my position. I knew I was going to catch this cat coming off the turn at 300 meters. As I stood behind my blocks everything that had come before that moment flashed through my mind. I heard those little kids at the Hartnell track telling me, "Alvin, you can do it. You can win the gold medal." I heard my little sister telling me how I could beat Michael Johnson. I was hearing things Calvin had told me. My mind was processing all of this as I stood there waiting to get into my blocks. I'm taking in all these images and I'm becoming more and more motivated. Of all the people in the world there, I was the one who could beat Michael Johnson. He was the one under pressure, not me. My heart wasn't beating like it had before during big races. I was calm. I just wanted to get it on. I knew I could go 43 seconds and I was ready to roll. I started putting my blocks together in the proper position. I was feeling great at that point. I saw my brother in the stands and waved to him. Then I got down into the blocks and I looked to the side. I catch Michael looking back at me. I knew I was on his mind. I put my head down to calm myself. I heard the command, "Runners to your mark." I'm telling myself, "This is what you've been waiting for. This is the moment you've been training for. This is it. It's all here right now." I took a deep breath, smiled and threw my head down. I'm thinking about coming off that first turn and seeing Michael struggling to catch me. That's the mental image I have in my mind as I wait for the gun. Pow! The gun goes off and I could hear the crowd start to roar. I saw cameras flashing all over the stadium. I saw Mike and Antonio get out quick so I know I have to run with the pack. I hear everybody breathing. I can hear all the footsteps. My senses are going crazy and I'm completely aware of everything going on around me. I hear the crowd getting louder and louder as we head for the top of the turn at 200 meters. I see Antonio Pettigrew start to make a little move so I make a small move at about 180 meters. Then I see Michael make his move at about 220 meters. I'm trying to calculate the exact moment he makes his move because I'm going to match him. I can't afford to make my move even five meters before Michael does because he'll have that much more energy. But I make my move too late and I know it. Now I pass Antonio and it looks like I might catch Michael, but he just maintains his pace. At 70 meters I know Michael's got it. I'm still trying to catch him and at 40 meters I look up to the screen and see Michael looking back at me. We run through the tape and I finished second. I'm disappointed because I wanted to win. I knew I could win. Immediately after the race I congratulate Michael and head toward the dressing room. On my way there all these fans are yelling, "Alvin, where are you going? It's a U.S. sweep of the first two spots. Go back out there." Then it dawns on me. Now I understand what happens to man and how we can get consumed with greed. Four years earlier I would have been ecstatic to win a bronze medal because I finished fourth. In 2000, I wasn't even happy with silver.

C A L V I N

I'm like a cannonball ready to explode after Alvin's race. I could not wait to run. I wanted to show everyone in that stadium I could run, too. But I didn't just want to win the gold medal. I really believed we had the team to break the world record in the 4 x 400-meter relay. I was so excited and so ready to run that I ran sub-44-second splits in each of the first two rounds.

A L V I N

I was actually more excited to be running the relay because I knew I'd be running with my brother. The 400 meters was all business, just me out there all alone. The relay was what I was waiting for. During the first two rounds Calvin ran the third leg and I was the anchor. In the first round you could feel the crowd starting to rise as Calvin approached me with the baton. He got about 50 meters from me and the roar started. It was like they were waiting for the same moment we were. They probably knew some of what we had been through in our lives. What they definitely knew was that there were two brothers in the Olympic Games, one handing off the stick to the other. As soon as he gave me that baton, the crowd just lit up.

CALVIN

It was like a dream come true. I had thought about that moment since 1996 when I saw LaMont Smith hand the stick to Alvin in the finals. At Sydney, Alvin's success in the 400 meters helped build the excitement for us in the relay. People knew who I was because we were brothers, but now they wanted to see me run.

ALVIN

Watching Calvin receive the baton in that first round felt like our crowning moment. When I saw him run I could feel the joy that comes from such a long wait. I knew everything he had gone through to get to that moment. It was like we were children again playing with the wind. I could see that same innocence, that same aura around him. And the crowd made it that much more special. As soon as I received the baton from Calvin I could feel this electrifying energy pass between us. That was the height of my experience in the Olympic Games. I look at that moment as our greatest achievement.

CALVIN

It was doubly good for me because not only was I able to run with my brother, but in the finals I got the chance to run with Michael Johnson. I'm the last guy to ever pass the baton to Michael in the 4 x 400-meter relay in the Olympic Games.

ALVIN

I realized in Sydney that our time is now. Those games closed the chapter for some athletes, but they opened a whole new book for Calvin and me. There is a reason we went back and forth between California and Florida. There is a reason we came back to California alone and then went to Orlando and found jobs on an assembly line and at Target. There is a reason we lived in a Mustang and picked ourselves up off those seats. We had to climb out of that car and face our destiny. There was no place to go at that point. But we arrived in Sydney. I know we can become the fastest runners ever in the history of track and field. If Michael Johnson can set world records in the 200 and 400 meters, we can definitely do the same thing

Now we understand just how sophisticated and technical track and field is at the world-class level. To one degree or another our entire lives revolve around what we are trying to accomplish on the track. We didn't have any idea of the depth to which we had to commit ourselves in 1996. From what we eat and when to how we conduct ourselves outside of practice, our goals and objectives demand an almost constant focus. Everything we do is part of a larger building process designed to have our minds and bodies prepared to peak at the appropriate time. In 2001 the target is July for the World Championships. In 2000 it was September for the Olympics. Our basic training is an example of this process and our depth of understanding compared to 1996. These are longer workouts at longer distances that generally start the preceding November or December. We'll run a series of long-distance sprints that start at 600 meters with a short rest period in between. We might do that on Monday and then come back on Tuesday for what we call a tempo run. It could be anything from one to two miles with the usual jogging and stretching before and after the workout.

The 400 meters is all about energy expenditure. That's why we are so focused on eating the right foods with the right combination of protein and carbohydrates. The entire process becomes extremely scientific. We are, for example, conscious of the length of our stride and whether or not our body is completely aligned. I'm to the point now where I can feel whether my neck or back is slightly out of line. I'll go to our chiropractor to have my spine realigned any number of times during the course of a season. We are conscious about replenishing our bodies after workouts and monitoring how we feel throughout the day with regard to food intake. I've found that eating something every two or three hours is the best way for me to maintain my energy levels. As far as the actual running, we know we run faster when we run right underneath our center of gravity as opposed to stretching out and taking longer strides. Technically, you want to be on the balls of your feet. Michael Johnson is the model image of how to run because he stays almost straight up over his center of gravity. We're able to watch ourselves run on film with a stick man, which is what we call the computer-generated character running alongside us. The stick man is there to show us how fast we could have run had we run more efficiently. Michael Johnson has assimilated the stick man into his form. It's become a part of him. That's something we are now just integrating into our running.

But a practice for us has as much to do with mental and spiritual preparation as the physical effort. We'll get to the track and just kind of settle into the surroundings. It doesn't matter whether it's the first time at that track or the 100th, we'll lie down in the grass and just kind of relax. As we've said before, we are naturalists. We really feel one with the physical environment, the wind, the ground, the trees. So there is a comfort in finding a place in the grass before we start our workout. We'll talk about what we're going to do that day, what our goals are for that workout. We're constantly using visual imagery to review what we are about to do and the level at which we want to execute those activities. If we're running 300 meters followed by 200 meters, then we might be looking to run 34 seconds in the 300 and 22 seconds in the 200. We might do a couple jogs on the infield with our shoes off to strengthen our feet and get

the blood circulating more freely. Then we often walk one or two laps on the inside of the track. Now we know exactly what we have to do to prepare ourselves.

A L V I N

Every runner has his or her own formula. Calvin and I have a very similar formula to prepare ourselves to run. We also have one another, which is the greatest asset anyone could have at this level. We're not just friends. We're tackling these goals and objectives together. We each want the other one to succeed at the highest level. There is no jealousy. We are two people working together as one unit. If we had grown up alone and without one another, we might not have reached the same level. But when I'm feeling down, Calvin is there to comfort me and when he's down, I'm there to comfort him. He's my strong hand when I'm weak and I'm his strong hand when he's weak. That's the way it's been since we were born and it's not something we take for granted. Both of us want to be world champions and the only way we can do that is to run two different events.

We want to create our own show. We can run the 400 or 200 and keep the rest of the world guessing. But we'll have a chance to be dominant in either event. We'll probably run together sometimes, but we'll concentrate on one or the other. Calvin went 20.50 in the 200 so I know he can go 19.5 with the proper technique and training. It's hard for people to judge my brother and me because they have never seen us over the course of three or four straight years. We were never stable enough to be consistent on the track. I know a lot of people looked at 1996 and wondered whether it was the real deal or just a fluke. They know we're the real deal now. We know our purpose at this time is to show people around the world something they haven't seen. It's just a matter of time. All the distractions we have encountered along the way have only made us stronger and more resilient. There isn't anything holding us back now.

I think we have a chance to become the future of track and field. With the proper training and focus, we could take the sport to the next level. I know we have the potential to break some world records. It's bound to happen because we have just scratched the surface of our abilities. I could see the 4 x 400-meter relay record going down. I could see the 200-meter record going down. I could see the 400-meter record going down. I could even see us testing the 100-meter record at some point. No man has ever run under 44 seconds in the 400, under 20 seconds in the 200 and under 10 seconds in the 100. Why not make that an objective? We have the opportunity to establish our own identity as the fastest sprinters on the planet. History is not going to stop with the current world records. They will be improved upon. I don't see a guy running a 40-second 400 meters. But I do see somebody running under 43 seconds. I can see a 42.89 and I think we can do that.

We have only given the world a taste. I've shown maybe a third of my capabilities. Calvin hasn't shown more than 25 percent of his potential.

C A L V I N

You have to remember that one second in the 400 meters is the difference between making a living and being a millionaire. One second can change our lives financially. But none of this is really about the money. We have a gift from God and it is our responsibility to use every ounce of that gift. That's why we are so focused and work so hard. We have the ability. The rest is up to us.

Right now the rest of the world thinks we're going to be running the 400 meters exclusively. I know there are guys out there who think they have the 200 meters all to themselves. We know what we can do at both distances. With the current era coming to a close, I don't think there is anyone out there who can beat us consistently if we follow our destiny.

A L V I N

My own personal goal is to be the fastest man in history.

C A L V I N

He'll be right behind me.